FINDING

Love

AFTER HEARTBREAK

VOLUME I

STEPHAN LABOSSIERE

Finding Love After Heartbreak, *Volume I*

Copyright ©2019 by Stephan Labossiere for Stephan Speaks, LLC

Published by Highly Favored Publishing

First Edition: March 2019

For information, contact Highly Favored Publishing –
highlyfavoredent@gmail.com

Editor & Creative Consultant: C. Nzingha Smith

Formatting: Ya Ya Ya Creative – www.yayayacreative.com

ISBN No. 978-0-9980189-4-2

PRINTED AND BOUND IN THE UNITED STATES OF AMERICA

$\mathcal{T}$ABLE OF $\mathcal{C}$ONTENTS

*I*NTRODUCTION

*Y*ou've hit rock bottom. You've experienced the soul-wrenching, devastating pain of losing someone you gave your heart to. You wake up every morning feeling like you've been hit by a truck. You don't know how to stop that hurt from washing over you every second of the day. It won't let up. You're scared to death you'll never heal, let alone, love again. It feels like free-falling. Hold out your hand. I can catch you.

I understand your pain. I understand every tough mountain you've had to climb for love. I've climbed the same mountains and had to fight the same tough battles. I know how hard it is to take a punch emotionally and try to get back up again. I know how hard it is to try to find the strength and energy to move forward, when you feel like you've been beaten down repeatedly. I know how difficult it is to trust love and life. I know what it's like to give so much of yourself and to not get what you hoped for, wished for, or felt you deserved in return. I know what it's like to experience being taken advantage of and for your efforts not to be appreciated.

If you've taken your first or thousandth stab at love and it ended in heartbreak, I want to take the jaded, I-should-have-known-better bitterness and turn it into an emotionally healthy will to love yourself and others again.

Unfortunately, love alone can't produce or sustain a relationship. You can't make someone love you. In order to love yourself or be ready to really love anyone else, you must first address any unresolved issues within you. A certain level of introspection is needed to allow you to evolve and attain freedom in love, rather than being locked down by the toxicity of negative emotions.

How do I know?

I know because I've been where you are. I've experienced what it feels like to think you'll never find the strength to love again. I also know that you, like me, can and will heal from your heartbreak.

Staying down is not an option. You need to get up. You need to heal. You must overcome this, and you will. You will because you have the strength in you to do it. I'm simply going to lay out the tools for you to accomplish what now feels like the impossible.

With a solid plan, intention, and consistent practice, you can learn how to open your heart again. You can also learn how to avoid the pitfalls that can affect your future relationships, including the one with yourself, which is the most important one of all. Dwelling in pain and hurt hinders your self-growth, which ends up negatively impacting all your other relationships.

Even though it doesn't feel good, heartbreak is the best reset button for your life. It's the opportunity for rebirth you've been waiting for, even if you weren't aware of it. Heartbreak lights a fire under you and pushes you to take the steps needed toward becoming a better version of yourself. Self-improvement is something we sometimes forget to do, when we're overly invested in someone else—or in their ghost—after a relationship ends.

It's very common for people to get into relationships that don't serve them and that aren't healthy because they're running from the work, they need to do on themselves. The relationship serves as a distraction because it's always easier to try to fix someone else than it is to work on fixing yourself.

However, every situation is a learning opportunity. What's done is done. It's important to use this time to find and empower yourself, even amid heartbreak. Your healing lies in the most heart-wrenching valleys of hurt. Valleys you'll need to face in order to overcome them and see the views from the mountaintops again.

I want to warn you in advance. Healing is tough. I cannot lie to you or sugar coat it. This process is not going to be easy. However, going through this process is going to be well worth it. Understand that I'm not just relaying information here, I'm walking with you through this process. I'm there with you, holding your hand. I'm going to support you every step of the way. Every emotion you're going to go through and experience, I understand because I've had to go through this same process myself. Trust me and we'll get through this together.

I don't want the negativity from your past experiences to hold you back any longer. That's what has happened. You've been held back. You've been hindered. You've suppressed your true self because you're afraid of being hurt again. No more.

I wrote this book to give you the tools you can use to overcome the emotional wasteland of heartbreak and free yourself from its ties, just like I managed to do.

I wrote this book to give you a rare and straightforward dose of the reality of working out your healing without the fluff. I wrote this book to teach you how to take the reins back in your life and your relationships, as well as how to harness and change your energy from negative to positive.

However, I didn't write this book to give you a bunch of recycled, generic, love advice that's been plastered all over fluffy magazines and websites. I didn't write this book to coddle you and keep you inside your comfort zone. Again, this process isn't going to be easy, but it will pay off if you're committed to going against the grain and doing the work required to get the results you desire.

We live in a society of perceived instant gratification. The norm has become filling emotional voids with substitutes, which makes it difficult to go against the grain. Going against the grain is hard. It takes courage to acknowledge the patience and hard work that this path to healing, self-discovery, and forgiveness towards yourself and others, requires. This is the main reason why so many others choose to numb their pain and claim they've "moved past it," when in fact, they're really stuck in the mud. Oblivious and unaware, they spend their wheels trying to figure out why they can't find happiness.

Not you. You are choosing differently. You actually want to be able to experience true happiness in life and lasting success in love. For that to happen, I need you to promise me, as you read this book, you're going to fully embrace everything in it and be an active participant in the exercises.

You're reading this book for a reason. Don't let the information I share with you go to waste. Don't let this opportunity pass you by.

If you do your part, you're going to see your life change for the better. You're going to see things go to a level you never, ever dreamed of. If you follow the instructions I lay out for you and complete each exercise honestly, you'll be able to experience the healing necessary to fully love yourself and be ready and open to love someone else.

Completing the Stephan Speaks Healing Method in its entirety will be the beginning of your freedom. This guide will be the beginning of your peace. Once completed, you'll have the skills you need to always bounce back from the unexpected punches of disappointment and heartbreak life throws your way. You will never stay down again. You'll never feel like you can't get up again.

After completing the steps in my healing method, you will know how to take life's punches as well as land some punches of your own. Swinging back at life, your punches communicate your strength and persistent will. Each punch says, "I'm not giving up. I'm going to get what's mine."

It's time to stop trying to cover up your wounds, disguise them, or pretend they don't exist. Putting a Band-Aid over a deep cut doesn't allow it to heal properly. It's time to let old wounds breathe. It's time to acknowledge the unresolved hurt you have inside you. The hurt needs time to air out. This is the only way an opportunity for healing can take place. A scab will form in the place of the wound and eventually fall off with time, unburdening you for good. There might be a mark left behind, but it will no longer hurt to touch it. The scar will serve as a reminder of what you were able to overcome and the battles you've won.

I wrote this book for you because I love you. I wrote this book to address a common occurrence, something we all have to face in life, heartbreak. I wrote this book to help you deal with the aftermath of heartbreak and to help you heal from it. I want to see you experience your best life and your truest love.

I want to help you find love after heartbreak. It's still possible for you.

$\mathscr{H}$ow $\mathscr{N}$ot to $\mathscr{G}$et
OVER HEARTBREAK

$\mathscr{B}$efore we jump into healing and how to find love after heartbreak, I want to be clear about a few things you shouldn't do in order to get over a current heartbreak.

GETTING UNDER SOMEONE TO GET OVER SOMEONE

Wrong. Wrong. Wrong. When you're quick to go find someone else to help you get over your heartbreak, all you're doing is turning a blind eye to what's going on within you. Nine times out of ten, if not ten out of ten, the person you get with, the rebound, will be the wrong person for you.

After a heartbreak, it's better for you to be alone. You aren't in the proper emotional state to handle a healthy, loving relationship. You aren't yet ready to be vulnerable again in a way that true love requires. So, you're going to end up jumping into the wrong relationship as a result.

You might be saying, "Who cares? I'm not looking for the right relationship. I just got hurt. I need companionship." I get it. In theory, it sounds good, but it's the wrong thing to do. It's understandable for you to want to seek comfort and to have someone be there for you. However, what you're not seeing is the danger you're running headfirst into.

Let's look at the angle of the situation being strictly casual. You go into it as a momentary thing. It's just something to help you get over the hump and you'll be fine. I can't tell you how many people have gone into these so-called "casual/temporary situations" and end up getting stuck for life. An unwanted pregnancy turns into a marriage proposal, for the sake of the baby, and into many years of unhappiness, resentment, and more hurt. All because you made a permanent decision based off a temporary situation.

Again, it seems harmless at first, but it's very easy to find yourself developing, in most cases, an unhealthy attachment to the individual. Because you're in a vulnerable state, you'll overlook many of their red flags and flaws. Those same red flags and flaws are going to come back to haunt you. Also, adding more damage to you over time. Finding someone to help you get over your heartbreak is going to create more problems you'll eventually need to heal from.

Another reason why this type of situation is not healthy is because now you're involving someone else in your web of pain. Running away from your hurt and into another "situation" only ends up hurting the other person. Now you're contributing to the "hurt people, hurt-people" cycle. So please, don't rush to get with anyone in order to get over your hurt. Don't do it. It's a setup for disaster every single time. Trust me.

SUPPRESSING YOUR FEELINGS

You might be the type of person who prides yourself on being strong. You try not to let anything bother you or at least you give the perception to people that nothing bothers you. The reality is you may in some ways move on quickly from hurtful situations. However, moving past hurt and healing are two different things. You're not resolving anything when you move past things in your mind, you're just suppressing your issues. In other words, you're simply "acting."

When you pretend and suppress your true feelings, holding onto hurt, it turns into emotional stress that will start to wreak havoc on your body. Emotional stress often manifests as illness and disease. I'll get more in depth with this in a later chapter. However, just know it's unhealthy in every area of your being to suppress your feelings.

There's nothing wrong with accepting how you feel and finding healthy ways to process your emotions. It's a matter of learning how to accept how you feel, instead of dismissing your feelings. You'll learn how to do this as you continue reading. Again, do not suppress your feelings. Ever. Again.

USING DISTRACTIONS TO COPE

People use distractions all the time. They add more to their plate to distract themselves from their deeper issues. You'll often here them use language like, "I'm so busy. I've just got too much going on."

Distractions only help you cope. They do not resolve or help you heal from your issues. Adding all these extra distractions to your already overloaded plate, only creates more stress in your life. Stress equals more anxiety, more unhappiness, and more discontentment. Essentially, you're doing more damage by trying to avoid or run from the hurt you experience, than good.

Bottom line, distractions are the wrong way to go. You don't want to look for distractions to cope with heartbreak. You want to refocus your life. Figure out what your issues are, that you undoubtedly need to home in on, and begin working on those things. This can include your physical health in general, emotional health, mental health, spiritual life, your career, your finances, etc.

Focusing on the work you need to do is not the same as staying distracted. Making improvements in your life should be done in a more goal-oriented way. Taking this approach helps you achieve what you actually want to have in life.

Take inventory of what you have going on currently. Be honest with yourself about what is truly necessary in your life right now. Create a balance by eliminating everything that doesn't align with the life you wish to create. Doing this will create more peace and space for you to grow. Distractions only create chaos and stress, keeping you unhealthy.

ONLY PRAYING ABOUT IT

Before you jump down my throat, let me explain. I am a man of God. I do believe in the power of prayer. I do believe praying is good and everyone should do it. However, I'm going to be very, very honest here. I see people all the time who think they can simply say a prayer without needing to do anything else. After praying they expect everything to be fixed and believe their work is done.

However, scripture states, *"Faith by itself, if it does not have works, is dead."* James 2:17, ESV

You can pray, but you must put work in with your prayers for them to be answered.

Your deeper issues aren't going to be resolved simply after saying a few prayers if you don't do anything else about them. You're praying and then wondering why nothing is happening. It's because there are still steps, you need to take that go along with your prayers and faith.

It's important you don't make this mistake. Use prayer not just to make a request unto God, but to seek God's guidance on how you need to move forward to resolve your issue(s) completely. Sometimes the work could include, going to a coach or counselor, in addition to following the steps I'm going to lay out in this book.

Whatever it is, there's always some extra work needed on your part, in addition to you praying about a situation. It's up to us to seek God to find out what steps we need to take in prayer and then follow God's direction. Many times, we're just speaking out loud, asking for things to be changed, but not doing anything within our control to help the situation. Then we get mad at God for not answering our prayers. This ends up being counterproductive and causing us to veer away from God, instead of nearer to Him, when we're in a troubled and broken state. Be mindful of this moving forward.

WAITING FOR
TIME TO HEAL YOU

I heard the saying a lot growing up, "Time heals all wounds." I think that's a bunch of nonsense. Time alone is not going to heal you. There are plenty of people who've gone to their graves still holding onto their deeper issues. They never healed. They never broke the cycle of hurt in their lives. Time, plus the work you put in, praying, taking the steps I'm going to lay out in this book, will heal you. However, time alone, will not heal you.

If you think living your life and moving forward in your mind will do the trick, I'm here to tell you, good luck. You'll wake up 20 years from now and realize, "Oh my gosh, I'm still hurt from something that happened to me when I was a child." Time will work with you to heal. However, it won't do the work for you. You still need to do what's required to make sure you experience the healing you need.

Now that you know what not to do, we can move on to the healthy actions you can and should take to heal yourself from heartbreak.

$\mathcal{S}$TEPHAN $\mathcal{S}$PEAKS
HEALING METHOD OVERVIEW

$\mathcal{O}$n your personal path to healing, you must commit to doing the work it takes to process through any unresolved pain and hurt lingering from your past. To help you do so, I've mapped out some of the things that helped me on my personal healing journey.

I believe the steps and exercises I'm going to share with you throughout this book will get you on your way to healing. I also realize that healing is a very personal process because everyone is at a different place in life and will need to work through different levels of pain and hurt.

However, the *Stephan Speaks Healing Method* allows you to go at your own pace, to work through things individually or collectively depending on your needs. I am here with you in spirit and truth as your guide to support you and encourage you along the way.

I want to encourage you to take your time. This is not a race. You aren't competing with anyone. You can do this solo or create a circle of people who might want to join you and offer additional support as you all walk toward being free, healed, and whole together. You're in control of this process. Only you truly know what's going to work best for you.

With that said, there are many methods you can take to heal. My healing process is a good way to begin or continue a previously started self-healing journey.

Using my approach to healing will enable you— if you do the work required—to become healthy and whole again. I say "again" because your natural state of being is whole and complete, not lacking anything. I want to help you get back to the authentic you, capable of giving and receiving the abundance and wonder of love you were meant to experience in your life.

THE PROCESS

There are seven steps to the *Stephan Speaks Healing Method*.

1. Put the hurt out in front of you

2. Getting things off your chest part I: speaking your truth

3. Getting things off your chest part II: letter writing release

4. Getting things off your chest part III: sending the letters

5. Practicing forgiveness

6. Changing your mindset

7. Trusting God, not people

We're going to explore each step thoroughly. You'll spend time working through each step at your own pace and personal level of comfort. I will lay out the necessary steps you'll need to take in each chapter in order to work out your healing.

Unlike my other books where you were able to sit back and be a receiver of insight and information, with this book, I'll need you to be an active participant. This book is meant to be an interactive experience for your benefit. None of what I share with you in this book is going to work for you, unless you're willing to do the work required to see the results.

GETTING STARTED

Before you dive in, if you haven't purchased the companion book, *Healing Heartbreak*, I highly recommend you go to my website, www.stephanspeaks.com now and order it. I've taken the time to lay it out in a way that compliments the exercises in this book. It's meant to help encourage and motivate you to stay on task while completing each step in your healing process.

However, if you aren't planning on purchasing, *Healing Heartbreak*, I recommend you buy a notebook or journal you use solely for completing the exercises in this book.

In addition to a workbook/journal, you'll need something to write with. A pen, marker, pencil, whatever works best for you. Keep it attached to your workbook/journal so it's always there when you need it.

You'll also need to schedule some blocks of quiet time to devote to reading and working through the healing exercises. Depending on your life and how busy you are, I would start by setting aside time early on a Saturday. Take out an hour or two at the beginning of your day, before you officially start to be "busy" to read and work through the exercises.

Again, this is up to you and should be based on what works best for you. You are in control here. The important part is that once you begin, you continue to make time to go back to it as needed. I need you to be consistent. Consistency is going to be key in working through your healing.

The only other thing you'll need is patience.

Chances are you've got a backlog of unresolved pain and hurt lingering within you that's going to take time to pinpoint and work through. As I mentioned earlier, this is not a race. The healing process is not something that can be rushed through. It will require as much time as it requires. Period.

Knowing this ahead of time, release the pressure on yourself associated with the need to create expectations. Simply embrace the unknown. Make the resolve that you're going to have to trust the process. Take the needed time, whatever that may look like for you.

I also want you to be patient with yourself from start to finish. You've probably never tried to really work through your issues before. It's going to feel uncomfortable and it's going to be challenging. Again, be patient with yourself. This is not an easy, quick fix. Your issues didn't all happen overnight. Meaning, they're also not going to disappear overnight.

Lastly, I want you to have courage through this process. I want you to be brave and honest with yourself. The truth can be difficult to come to terms with. It requires courage to be honest with yourself when things come up that you've put forth an effort not to have to deal with. It's okay. You can do this.

Remember, I'm here with you every step of the way. Praying for you. Encouraging you. Cheering you on.

Be strong and courageous and do the work.
Do not be afraid or discouraged,
for the Lord God, my God, is with you.
–I CHRONICLES 28:20, NIV

POSSIBLE SIDE-EFFECTS

On your healing journey, which can be looked at as the equivalent of an emotional and spiritual cleanse/detox, you need to be aware of the possible side-effects you might experience as a result of committing to a process that's good for you.

You can expect to experience large amounts of doubt. Doubt in the process and its validity. Doubts in yourself and your ability to complete the process. Doubts of whether it will be worth it in the end. All these are healthy. All your doubts can be proven wrong if you continue the process through to the end. You will have crushed those doubts and gotten the answers and results you want and are hoping for.

Other side effects might include, strong emotional reactions to the truths you discover along your healing journey. Allow them. They are healthy. They are a part of your detox and cleansing. They are the necessary releases you need to get to the healed version of yourself.

Despair or discouragement throughout the process might show up as well. Judgement and the need to place blame. Temporary sadness is possible.

All these things I will help you process through. When they come up, if you feel yourself wanting to quit or stop prematurely, I encourage you to pray this short prayer, *"God, I give all my worries and cares to you, for I know and trust that you care about me."* It's derived from the scripture, I Peter 5:7, NLT

Allow whatever comes to come. Don't try to control it. It's a part of the process. Listen, I need you to do me a favor. Trust the process. Trust me. Trust yourself. Most importantly, trust God. This is what you need. You must clear out the unhealthy for the healthy to shine through. You've got this. God has you.

> *"We often resist what we most need."*
> –JULIA CAMERON

Pay attention to the resistance you feel as you're working through the exercises. Know and be encouraged when you experience it because it means you're making progress and you're getting what you need from this process.

It's also important to note here that going through a detox is often not a pretty thing. It can get ugly. Nasty stuff comes out of you. However, the detox is going to give way to the healthy, radiant, gorgeous, most beautiful within you. This detox is going to do wonders for your outward appearance and overall vibe. So, give yourself as many passes as you need so that you don't get caught up in how it appears or how you look as you're going through it. I want you to have just as much inward beauty as you do outwardly.

"As within, so without."
–HERMES TRISMEGISTUS

RESULTS

Results will vary.

You're in complete control of the results. Even though I lay out the information that I know will get you on the path to your healed self. It's also entirely up to you how much you get out of this self-healing process.

If you want the best results, you'll need to commit to doing your best throughout the entire process. Completing all the exercises and taking all the steps I lay out. Then, once you've finished reading the book and doing the exercises, you'll need to commit again to implementing what you learned on your healing journey into your everyday life.

You will need to take the principles, insight, and information, and apply them practically. You'll have to make the decision to change your habits, thoughts, words, and perceptions to align with what's going to best serve you overall in life and in your relationships, which are positivity and love.

Healing yourself and operating from a place of wholeness is a choice and practice that you will need to make and stay committed to. What we practice becomes our habits. Our habits become our behavior. Our behavior becomes our character. Our character is who we are below the surface. Choose to go deep and you'll get the best results.

$\mathscr{I}$'M $\mathscr{C}$OMMITTED
CONTRACT

I _____, understand that I am about to undertake an intensive, guided encounter to self-healing. I understand that the information and process of the Stephan Speaks Healing Method will go in detail as to how I can begin my healing journey and cleanse and detox the unresolved hurt and pain that has been lingering in my life.

I _____, commit myself to doing the work. I will take the necessary time out daily or weekly to read each chapter and complete the exercises and steps with the process that Stephan shares with me for my benefit.

I, _____, also understand that this guided self-healing process will allow me to work through any negative emotions and feelings that I need to deal with in order to experience complete healing. I, _____, commit to being kind and loving to myself during this process. I will be patient and understanding with myself and others as I work through the steps. I will take breaks if needed, but I am committed to being consistent and courageous through to the end.

_____
    Signature

                                       _____
                                         Date

How Early Experiences
WITH HEARTBREAK SHAPE US

MY STORY

At 15, my three sisters and I began to worry that our father was sleeping with another woman. As our suspicions grew in our minds like a virus, my second oldest sister, Rachel, was determined to find out the truth behind this mystery that was eating us alive. Even though I sensed it was more true than false, I would have preferred to stay in denial than to face it.

Rachel didn't agree with my position. She preferred to know the truth. I felt better in the dark. I didn't want to have to deal with the reality of it, if it was true.

The opportunity we sought to act on our suspicions came when my mother left to go out of town for work. Once she left, we noticed that our father had also disappeared. Only, he wasn't traveling for work. Rachel was sure she knew where he was. We devised a plan on how to get the answers we needed and uncover the truth.

My high school friend, Terry, owned a big blue van. I convinced him to drive us past the house my sister thought my dad would be. He agreed. I remember, my three sisters, myself, and a few other friends hopping into Terry's van and riding past the house my sister Rachel insisted on, to see if my dad's car was there.

Our ugly suspicions were immediately confirmed as we rounded the block and saw my dad's car parked in the driveway of a house belonging to a woman, we'd seen in passing around our neighborhood. It was late. His car was there. Everyone put the pieces of the puzzle together. We now had our proof.

Mentally, I think I blacked out at that moment. I honestly don't remember if anyone said anything once we got a safe distance away from the house. I don't know if Rachel gave herself kudos for solving the mystery. Nothing. The sudden, devastating fact that my dad was seeing another woman was too much for me to process. I became numb to everything going on around me.

One thing was for sure, we assumed our mother didn't know. We wracked our brains, trying to figure out how to deal her this devastating blow. Rachel was adamant about letting my mother know the truth, no matter how harsh it would be. So, keeping this secret between us was out of the question.

Rachel decided she was going to tell our mother about our suspicions and our proof once she arrived back from her trip. I decided I didn't want to be involved in the process of telling my mom the news. I was prepared to lock myself in my room upon my mother's return.

The night my mother returned from her trip was without question the most unforgettable night of my life. I wasn't sure when or how Rachel broke the news to her. However, I remember being in my room, watching TV, purposely distracted, when out of nowhere my mother bursts in sobbing.

She reached for me and held me tight. I hugged her back as tightly as I could to comfort her. In our embrace, and through her tears, she admitted that she already knew about the affair. She confessed that she always knew. She kept his secret in order to protect us from its painful reality.

At the time I was just a teenager. I didn't know what to do or how to feel about the situation. There was a time shortly after the affair came out when my dad and I were alone. He was driving me to a friend's house and he blurted out, "I really do love your mom," as if I had posed the question to him and he was responding.

Honestly, his confession made me feel awkward. I almost felt like none of it was my business. I didn't know what to do with the information. I didn't really know how to process any of what was going on. I didn't know how to feel about it. Unconsciously, I made the decision not to feel anything. I simply didn't want to deal with it. So, I suppressed the my emotions without even knowing it.

Fast forward. When it was all said and done, my parents did stay together and eventually worked it all out.

However, the damage my father's affair caused lingered, negatively altering my outlook on love and relationships. I honestly didn't know how devastating this experience would ultimately become for me until I was a man. Even though I was outside of my poor mother's hurt, it shaped my early perception of love, relationships, and commitment, entirely. I just couldn't understand how someone who truly claimed to love another human being could muster up the cruelty to betray them in that way. I really felt bad for my mother for having to deal with cheating. The whole time I was sympathizing with her pain, not realizing my own or acknowledging how the situation truly affected me.

It wasn't until much later in my life that I had to face the fact that witnessing my mother's hurt, created a negative perspective of relationships for me. This negative perception fed all my early relationships with a toxic fire that burned them alive, one after the other. Unbeknownst to me at the time, this early experience of heartbreak, even as a witness, doomed my impending relationships.

I made a promise to myself at 15 to never be unfaithful to anyone I cared about. From my mother's experience, I had developed a true fear of hurting people. Out of this fear, came a hypersensitivity to other people and an obsession with not wanting to cheat on women. After seeing my mother's pain, I was sure I never wanted to hurt anyone I loved like that.

Little did I know, I would allow this fear to grow out of control. To keep me from exploring potential relationships with people I genuinely cared for and that might have had the potential to grow into sustainable, loving relationships.

Operating from this extreme place of fear, kept me guarded, frustrated, and angry. It kept me in a negative mindset and it ultimately kept love away. I paid a very high price for not wanting to acknowledge or deal with my pain and hurt from this early experience. However, at the time, I wasn't sure how to. I learned. You can too.

PART I

UNDERSTANDING

Pain

HAS ITS BENEFITS

$\mathcal{T}$HE $\mathcal{T}$RUTH $\mathcal{A}$BOUT
BEING HURT

$\mathcal{I}$deally, it would be great if we were able to choose the things we had to go through in life. We would probably choose not to go through anything that was unpleasant, hurtful, or that caused us pain at all. We would choose to only experience the amazing, wonderful things life offers like happiness, joy, and being in mutually loving, healthy, blissful relationships.

Unfortunately, that's not how life works. We can't handpick all our experiences. As we live our lives, we will all have to endure hurtful experiences. As adults, it's probably safe to say that we've all been let down and hurt by love before. We've all been disappointed at one point or another by someone we loved, and it's bound to happen to us again in the future. This is just a fact of life. There's no getting around it. We're all going to experience tough times and face obstacles that seem daunting and maybe even impossible to get over, when we're in them.

Hurt is undoubtedly one of the most inescapable things in life. Since this is the case, it's important to understand and learn more about the phenomenon of being hurt. By not understanding the impact of hurt on our lives, we allow hurt to get the best of us. We allow hurt to beat us down and put us in a negative headspace. We allow hurt to hold us back and paralyze us in life. If we stay ignorant to our hurt and its effects, all these things will simply continue to work against us.

Getting a full understanding of what hurt involves will allow you to resolve your past hurt. You'll also be able to conquer any future hurt you face. You will no longer be afraid of being hurt. Instead you'll be prepared for hurt when it strikes. You will know how to handle yourself as a result of getting a proper understanding of why we go through certain experiences.

PAIN

Pain is the emotion we feel when we experience a hurtful situation. Pain, like hurt is also an inevitable part of life. Pain can manifest as both physical and emotional once we've gone through a hurtful experience.

One of the biggest disservices you can do to yourself and even your children, if you have them, is to try to shield them from getting hurt. You might be the type of parent that'll try to stop their child from experiencing anything too hurtful to their feelings. I'll use the subject of participation trophies as an example.

Now, I'm not here to argue a position on whether participation trophies are right or wrong. I know some people feel strongly about the benefits of participation trophies. However, in the context of this discussion, one of the reasons why people believe in participation trophies is because they're trying to shield their child from the feelings of disappointment and pain. They don't want their child to be letdown or feel they're not good enough because they weren't able to accomplish their goal of winning.

Losing at anything is a blow to a person's self-esteem and it's understandable why a parent or guardian would want to keep their child away from having to experience this pain. As a parent they feel their job is to protect their child from as many negative experiences as possible.

However, this does more harm than good in the long run. When you don't let your child go through the process of being hurt and processing through painful emotions, as your child grows older, they won't know how to deal with disappointment or rejection. They won't know how to deal with hurt and pain in a productive way. They also won't understand how to deal with the reality of situations. In some circumstances, they won't be good enough in certain areas.

When I say, "not good enough," it's not in a way to beat you or your child up. I say it in a way to help you make the connection and understand that your child isn't going to be suited for every single activity they pursue.

Every person is not meant to be a football player. Every person is not meant to be an actor, a singer, an engineer, a doctor. You get my point here. Sometimes disappointments happen to help a person better see where their strengths lie or where improvement is needed in order to accomplish their goals. This is healthy. Both insights are good and very beneficial to have in life. It saves you time, energy, money, and frustration. You can then focus your resources on the areas and activities they're best suited for.

Since hurt is inevitable and we're all going to experience hurt throughout our lives, it's honestly pointless to try to avoid it. Instead, it's more important to learn the truth about being hurt so you're better equipped to handle it when it comes. I want to teach you how to handle it better going forward.

However, before I go any further, I want to point out that I don't want you to expect to get hurt in every situation or develop a cynical attitude around hurt. If you do, you'll walk around dejected with a negative vibe, which will also work against you. This is counterproductive. You don't need to expect to get hurt. However, I want to prepare you for it, so when it happens to show up, you don't get caught off guard every time.

Being prepared and being paranoid are two different things.

Listen, I don't want you to feel like you need to run from pain. Running from hurt and disappointment doesn't teach you how to deal with it. Every time hurt, or pain comes your way, it gives you an opportunity to learn how to better deal with it. You can then begin to see and understand what lessons each experience is supposed to teach you.

Pain and hurt are teachers. The lessons they teach, even though uncomfortable, are lessons we need to be willing to accept. The lessons help make us better people. They build our character, confidence, and help us to be better prepared for the trials of life we have yet to face.

Understand that in getting hurt, you always have a choice. You can either stay down and stay hurt or you can decide to take the necessary steps to recover. You can get back up again. You have the ability, whether you realize it or not, to overcome any pain thrown your way.

Now granted, when we're going through it, it doesn't feel like we have any choices at all. It often feels like the end of the world. It feels like, "Oh my gosh. How am I ever going to get past this? How am I ever going to recover?" In the moment, the pain blinds you and blocks your ability to see past the situation, to a better place.

Understand that whatever you're going through isn't the end for you or your life. It's so important for you to remember this is a reset period. This is a new opportunity for you to position yourself for the greater to come in your life. It all starts with you making the decision to get back up again. You were able to take the punch. You survived and are surviving it, even now. You can decide to recover and get back up from it.

Again, I know it sounds easier said than done, but I want to encourage you. It doesn't help you to stay focused on the fact that it's hard. It is hard. It's also understandable when we want to stay stuck in these moments for prolonged periods of time. However, it's more important for us to fight through those moments so they don't last a lifetime.

MY EXPERIENCE

No one is exempt from pain, including me. It's easy to think that because I'm able to help other people deal with their relationship issues that I, myself, don't often need to take my own advice.

I want to share with you what I do, personally, regarding bouncing back from hurt and disappointment. It could be pain and disappointment in my career, my relationships, or my physical fitness goals. Whatever area of my life that disappointment shows up, I give myself permission to have a grieving period of three days.

Here's what my grieving period looks like under normal circumstances.

Day 1: There are no rules. I give myself permission to have a full-blown pity party. I view day one as an opportunity to acknowledge the hurt I feel from whatever happened to me. You can't move past anything in life without first facing it and acknowledging how it makes you feel. Your feelings are valid.

I'm human. I don't need to pretend nothing ever phases me. It does. It's healthy for me to be honest about how I feel and how things affect me.

Giving yourself permission to be honest about what happened and how it affected you is the first step in being able to move forward without allowing those negative feelings to linger. You don't want them to end up being suppressed and unresolved.

I don't wave away or dismiss my hurt or pain. I face it. I look at it. I give myself and my emotions the respect we both deserve in that space.

Day 2: I give myself permission to mourn whatever happened. Feelings of grief are a natural response to pain, hurt, and loss. Normally there is some feeling of loss felt when you experience hurt and it's important to process through it. I allow myself to feel sad, disappointed, angry, frustrated, and so on.

It's usually a combination of mixed emotions. I work through those emotions and resist the need to hold them in. I know that it's better to get them out of my system, so they won't keep me stuck over the long run.

It's good to mourn. It's good to grieve. You need it. It's healthy. You need to take time as soon as things happen to process through them. Don't wait.

The last thing you want to do is suppress things. You shouldn't feel like you must suppress how you feel about what goes on in your life.

If you're a man reading this, listen, I know many men are raised to suppress and hold back their feelings. We're told to suck it up and be tough, but it's not healthy. Now, that doesn't mean it's healthy being an emotional wreck 24/7 either. It just means you need to give yourself permission to learn how to deal with and process your feelings. Learn how to be honest about how you feel because that's going to help you bounce back from the pain and hurt.

Okay, so the first day is set apart to acknowledge what happened and be honest about my feelings and to just feel however I feel. The second day is set aside to grieve, mourn, and process through my emotions and how I feel about the situation without judgment.

Day 3: On the third day I begin to muster up the strength to pull myself out of grief. I'll be honest with you, sometimes it's the hardest thing to do because it's easier to sit and wallow in self-pity. Wallowing in misery is a useful distraction when you don't want to face what happened and how you feel.

However, since on day one and two, I faced my feelings instead of suppressing them, I now must decide to start working my way back into a healthier headspace. For me, this means, if I skipped working out on day one and two, by day three I make the resolve to go to the gym. Even if I don't get a full workout in, it's important that I put myself back into my normal routine. I get back to work. I begin to participate in the activities that make me feel productive and add to my sense of well-being.

For you, this could mean that if you spent the first two days eating away your feels and not sleeping properly, by day three, you need to make the decision to get back to eating healthier, spending time with family or friends, getting a workout in, etc. Start doing the things you do regularly that make you feel good and bring a smile to your face.

We tend to do things that compound our issues and make us feel worse when we're going through tough times emotionally, these include: not getting enough sleep, eating poorly, and not staying hydrated. All these things work to help us feel even worse. They zap the little strength we need to help us bounce back and pull ourselves up and out of the grief we feel from the pain we've experienced.

By the third day, it's important to start getting back into a healthier space. You do this by eating well, drinking plenty of water, and getting enough rest. It takes physical strength to pull yourself back up and keep going. If you don't, it's easy to keep wallowing in the unhealthy place. You tend to make unhealthy choices when you're grieving. So, you must make the decision to actively choose to do better.

Once my three-day grieving period is over, that's it. Time's up. I decide to get up, get back to work, and get focused again. It's all about my deciding to use the time wisely during my small grieving window. I acknowledge the hurt, allow myself to feel, process through my pain, grieve, and do my best to get it all out of my system in that time frame.

Decide what your process will be and the max number of days you think you'll need to go through your grieving process. Once you decide on a good time period for you, stick to it. Once your grieving period is over, it's done. Wipe the tears and make the decision to move forward. It doesn't mean you won't still have your moments. Deciding to move forward, simply means you aren't going to consistently dwell in the hurtful, broken place.

In more serious situations, like a passing in the family, being diagnosed with an illness, or something just as serious, you might need to take more time. Again, no one's expecting you to be perfect with this. However, set a time and once the time is up, make the decision to move on.

I keep emphasizing moving on despite the situation because there is danger in giving yourself too much leeway on your time frame. You can get to the point that you stay stuck. The one thing I've learned about being hurt is the longer you wallow and dwell in it, the harder it becomes to get out of that headspace. Believe it or not it's very easy to become comfortable feeling sad and depressed.

Let me be clear here, comfortable doesn't mean you're happy because clearly if you're wallowing in self-pity or sadness, there is no happiness there. However, you can still become very comfortable living in an unhappy state of being. It can become easy to remain in grief and find other methods of coping with it, like drugs, alcohol, sex, or porn. The coping list is endless.

Understand that there is a big difference between coping and healing.

All the things I just named are simply ways to temporarily deal and function, but they won't cure your hurt. When you choose to cope rather than take the steps needed to heal, you're piling more issues on top of your original issue or source of pain. Don't do it. Choose to heal instead.

Even when you give yourself a grieving period, it's not like life stops and waits for you. Life still goes on. It doesn't matter what happens. Life goes on. If you have children, your children still need you. You still need to earn a living. You still need to show up and be an active participant in your life.

Lastly, remember, "what does not kill you, makes you stronger." I know you've heard this saying a million times before. However, maybe you've never really processed or grasped the meaning behind it. Take a second and really think about it.

When you're able to endure something and then recover from it, a sickness, an emotional trauma, or anything else significant, you become stronger. You can check your pulse now to make sure, but if you're reading this, then you're still alive. You made it through. You faced whatever "it" is, even though you probably didn't think you could. Now, going forward, if this type of situation reoccurs, you're better equipped to handle it.

When your body gets attacked by a virus, then heals, your body is going to be better prepared if that sickness ever tries to come back and attack it again. The same is true if you've ever been mentally bankrupt before. In that first experience you might have panicked, fell into depression, or didn't know how to deal with it, but somehow you found your way out of it, and got back on your feet. Now, if you face mental burnout again, you are so much more equipped to handle it and can be confident you can conquer it again.

When you have a track record of going through and coming out, you're a winner at life. Begin to look at your life from this perspective. When you win at things you tend to develop a much calmer disposition because it's like, "You know what? I've been here before. I will get out of it again." You'll know how to handle it.

Everything is about perspective. When you look at each situation as a win because you went through it and came out, you'll begin to see there's a great upside to what you go through. Flip it. Turn the experiences you once viewed as losses into what they really are meant to be, lessons. You take some of your power back when you begin to flip the scenarios around. So, again, it's not about just saying what sounds like a feel-good saying meant to help you feel better in the moment. It's to remind you of who you are. You are powerful beyond measure.

A victim mindset is a choice. Since you can choose to see yourself as a victim or a professional a** whooper, which would you prefer?

Focus on the win. Focus on the fact you made it through your hurtful experiences, rather than giving so much power to the experiences. Granted, none of us wants to endure the hurt to get the lessons. I know it's hard to say to yourself, "Well, I guess there's a reason why it happened." However, this is how you build up your strength and confidence in facing future obstacles.

Sure, no one ever wants to have to go through pain in order to experience any pleasure, but the reality is:

that's usually how it works for most people. However, the people who are resilient are also usually able to get to a higher level in their lives because of the turmoil and the obstacles they overcame.

No storm lasts forever. On the other side of it is sunshine. There are going to be better days. You must keep walking and moving forward to see them.

Decide. Follow through. Get to the finish line.

When you do, you're going to see that what didn't kill you, did in fact make you stronger. You're going to be able to learn from the experience if you take a step back to evaluate things. Also, know that the valuable lessons you gain from each experience are not just for you. The lessons can help the people around you. Your friends, family, children, co-workers, and peers can all benefit from your experiences. Your lessons will help you help others.

Remember, it's not just about you.

Hurt People,
HURT PEOPLE

"Hurt people, hurt people." These are four of the truest words ever spoken.

We live in a world actively engaged in an extreme, ongoing negative cycle of existence. Damaged, hurt, broken people are passing their damage, hurt, and dysfunctional brokenness onto each another.

Parents pass it on to their children. Wives to their husbands. Husbands to their wives. Friends to their friends. Acquaintances to each other. Strangers to other strangers. Everyone is just passing around negative energy caused from unresolved hurt and a lack of healing. The brokenness comes out directed at others, usually the people closest to you.

Sometimes the passing on of hurt happens maliciously. It can also happen without a person knowing their doing it. However, one way or another, the hurt seeps out of them and into others. It's creating a society overcome by negativity and it's not a coincidence. It's not just coming out of nowhere. No. A bunch of hurt people are congregating together and in the process they've become unhappy. Most people don't think they're apart of the unhealthy bunch because there are different levels of brokenness and unhappiness people occupy. Some people are much more broken than others.

However, hurt people usually gravitate toward and congregate together. Doing so makes it easier to pass their hurt onto each other. Even people who don't think they're engaging in hurtful behavior, usually are. There is always more than what meets the eye. I'll explain what I mean in more detail, but first, I want to share some basic principles about healthy people.

A healthy person is someone who isn't holding onto a lot of negative energy. Negative energy can show up as a bad attitude, irritability, crankiness, defensiveness, or even being overly arrogant. Mainly because arrogance is usually a sign of insecurity or deeper issues present in a person. When you're showing any of those qualities on a regular basis, you're not healthy.

A healthy, happy person in general usually doesn't exhibit these types of behaviors. They're not rude and combative, always on the lookout for a fight or altercation of some kind.

A healthy person isn't going to be so quick to look at life, people, and situations from a negative perspective. A healthy person is going to look for the good in the situation as opposed to the bad. They're going to side on the side of optimism as opposed to pessimism. When you're always quick to assume the worse, jump to negative conclusions, or have a negative outlook on situations, this is evidence that there are deeper issues present within you.

A healthy person is going to be more patient with people. They aren't going to be so quick to find reasons to be offended by the actions of others. They see the good in others and actively choose to put their good out in front of them when interacting with other people. They are calmer and have more peace within them to extend to others.

An unhealthy person is naturally more combative, high-strung, and easily offended.

Healthy people don't purposefully do hurtful things to others. Granted, it's very possible a healthy, whole person might do something to hurt someone else without knowing it. At the end of the day, no one is perfect. No matter how much we think we understand things, or we think we're loving, wonderful people, our ignorance, our lack of understanding or sensitivity for how something may impact someone else, can lead us to engaging in behaviors that create issues.

I'm not going to knock anyone for that. The key is to simply accept that even when you don't mean to be offensive or hurtful toward others, it can happen. Now, don't get me wrong. I do feel like we live in a society prone to prematurely taking offense to almost anything. Even when you truly try with all your heart to speak or to engage in ways that aren't offensive, someone is going to be offended.

When you speak the truth, expect someone to be offended because people don't like the truth. However, there's a difference between someone internalizing or taking things absolutely the wrong way and you really doing something hurtful to someone. It's possible you didn't have a full understanding of your actions. However, it also goes back to the point that hurt is inevitable. No matter what we say or do, even when it's not meant to be hurtful, it can hurt someone. However, to reiterate my point here, healthy people don't go around doing hurtful things knowingly to others.

Examples of the "hurt people, hurt people" theory are evident throughout our lives in different forms. The theory can be seen when you're dealing with or have dealt with a neglectful parent. When dealing with a disrespectful romantic partner. When you engage with a stranger who seems to be lashing out at you for no apparent reason. Healthy, whole people don't do these things. Plain and simple.

A healthy, happy, person is not going to purposely be neglectful towards their child. They're going to be much more in tune with their child and much more understanding of what their child needs.

A healthy, whole, person isn't going to be disrespectful to their romantic partner. They aren't going to dismiss his/her feelings or make them feel insignificant in any way. Again, they'll be more in tune with their partner. They'll be more loving and sensitive to their partner's needs. A healthy, whole, stranger isn't going to lash out at another stranger. That's not how healthy people behave.

When you experience hurtful and unhealthy situations, understand that the person's behavior is coming from a place of unresolved hurt and pain.

Let me be clear here. I'm not validating the behavior of unhealthy people. In no way am I saying hurtful behavior is acceptable or okay. My goal here is to help you to understand the truth of where the behavior comes from. Let me give you an example to further illustrate my point.

I used to work at a call center, in a customer service role. One of the main principles they taught us was to not take things personally. When an irate customer called and went off on me, I knew it wasn't about me. It had nothing to do with me or anything I did or didn't do. Many times, they were angry at the company or they were upset the product didn't work. They might have been having a bad day. Whatever it was, it wasn't about me!

This goes beyond working in customer service or in a public facing job where I had to handle this type of situation on a regular basis. This principle is a life lesson we all need to learn. "Don't take anything personally." Understand that when someone is going off on your or being disrespectful, you're dealing with a hurt person. Don't take it personal. Don't internalize a person's rude behavior because if anything, they need help.

In my customer service experience and life in general, I've learned that the best way to defuse the situation is to simply help them. Now granted, I'm not sitting here telling you that you need to help every hurt person who comes at you sideways. Sometimes, it won't be your place to offer them help. Even if you do try to help, some people will reject your help because they don't even want to help themselves. You can't help someone who doesn't want to help themselves.

Again, don't take it personal. Don't internalize it. Understand they are engaged in the cycle of hurt people, hurt people.

Let me tell you what you can do for them regardless of whether they want your help or not.

Consider their pain and pray for them. Listen, you may not consider yourself to be super spiritual, but in the Bible, it tells us how we should even pray for our enemies. When someone is hurting you, even if it's a loved one, someone you truly care about, in that moment they might feel like your enemy. Praying for them in the moment will help you control yourself and keep you from engaging in the hurt people, hurt people cycle.

The last thing I want you to do is engage in unconstructive, negative behavior. Don't pour anymore negativity into them. That's where we go wrong in a lot of situations. Someone comes at us in a negative way, does something hurtful, and to defend ourselves we lash back out at them. We try to hurt them in return. We pour more negativity into an already negative situation. What happens as a result? The situation goes from bad to worse.

Now they're even more hurt than they were before. You're hurt and riled up. You get stressed out. Nothing good comes from it. So, again, instead of choosing to lash back out at them, consider their pain instead. When I say, consider their pain, ask yourself: "Where is this coming from? Why are they lashing out?"

Again, depending on the situation, it might not be your place or responsibility to completely process all of that. However, do your best to consider their pain before you react. They're speaking and engaging in this behavior from a place of hurt. It has nothing to do with you. Say to yourself, "I'm not going to take this personally. I can walk away." Then proceed to detach from the situation. If someone is coming at you in a negative and hurtful way and you address it properly, in a calm, positive manner, the best decision at that point is to detach from the person and situation.

If you're in relationship you don't belong in and this scenario fits your situation with your partner, it will mean ending your relationship. If you're dealing with family members that are always negative, it'll mean detaching from those family member(s). Maybe not for good, but at least until things can be handled in a more mature and loving manner on their part. It doesn't make any sense to continue to engage with anyone who is a source of negativity in your life.

I'll give you a personal example. When I post videos and positive messages on social media, I usually get tons of negative comments. One thing I've learned and what I want you to begin practicing if you engage in social media and get negative comments—especially if you're an influencer or someone who has a large number of followers—don't engage with negative people. To be more accurate, don't engage with hurt people.

These people are hurting. So, what do they do? They lash out at you on the Internet. They leave a bunch of nasty comments. When you engage with someone who has no intentions of trying to calm themselves down, think logically, or separate from their negativity, at least in the moment, you get pulled into a never-ending battle you can't win. It'll only bring you to a bad place.

Whether you realize it or not, you take on the other person's hurt from the situation. Whether you'll admit it or not, you end up hurt from the negative comments or behavior of others. You end up hurt from their attacking you and coming at you negatively. Trust me, you'll take it out on someone else.

When I see a negative comment, I simply don't respond. I either delete the comment or I just leave it alone and keep it moving. I've learned that it's not good to let yourself get sucked into negative situations. I pray for these people. I'm not saying this just to say it either. I'm serious. I'll sit at my computer or on my phone and after reading the comment, I'll say a prayer for the person. Hoping that whatever is causing them to behave in a nasty and negative manner gets resolved.

Whether it be negativity on the Internet or from family and friends, whatever it is, start to recognize when it's best to detach yourself from a person. If no genuine progress can be made to get to a calmer, better, and more loving place with them, it's time to walk away. Again, the door can always be opened to reconciliation and coming back together when the person is willing to come correct. Until then, it's not your duty to be a punching bag for anyone. Pray for people and keep it moving. Also, remember not to take what someone else does or says to you, personally.

My next point is equally important. Whether you realize it or not, you're hurting people too. Again, what is the saying? "Hurt people, hurt people."

You might be thinking "Well, I don't go around hurting people. I don't go around doing this or that. I'm hurt and I never did XYZ." It's bull.

You think you're not hurting people? You think you're not doing anything negative toward others? You have no idea. You have no idea how holding on to unresolved pain has caused you to pass it on to other people. Granted, you may not consciously engage in malicious behavior with the intent to hurt someone, but unknowingly, you do pass your negative energy on to others.

There are mothers and fathers right now who don't even realize how much negativity they've passed on to their children. The same children who are now adults. Who are now my clients and other helping professionals' clients. They have these tense, awkward, negative relationships with you as a result. Even though they may still talk to you every single day, they have also been deeply hurt by you in some way. Again, the hurt may not have been direct, malicious behavior.

When you're hurting, you become blind to how you impact other people. A hurt person gets so caught up in protecting themselves and their own feelings that they miss seeing what they're doing to other people.

It's important not to internalize what someone did to you. Whether you realize it or not, they were acting out of self-defense. For example, do you know someone who is always quick to criticize everyone else? They point out everyone else's flaws and will go in on other people. So much so, you'd think they did no wrong themselves.

Do you know the real reason for their behavior? It's not their desire to beat other people down. They just don't want to have the spotlight on them. Their mentality, whether it be conscious or subconscious, is "I'm going to hit everyone before they can hit me. I'm going to make it about everyone else, so they don't even have time to make it about me." If they make it about everyone else, they validate and excuse away any of their flaws that might be pointed out. The minute you even try to say anything to them, what do they do? They get defensive and deflect.

Again, they aren't behaving this way because they want to purposely go around hurting people. In their mind, they don't think they're engaging in the hurt people, hurt people cycle. However, this is a perfect example of how people constantly spread negativity, hurt, and pain by speaking against and down to others. Ultimately, if you're in their sphere of influence, it will have a negative impact on you.

Hurting others happens in various forms. Passing down negative energy is one way of hurting other people because you're putting them in a bad mindset and disrupting their positive energy flow. Your negative energy impacts their ability to focus and stay positive and happy throughout their day. All these things end up hurting them. Again, whether you realize it or not, you are passing your hurt on to other people.

It's imperative you commit to going through this process of healing. Collectively we all need to do our part to get better in order to stop the never-ending cycle of negativity.

Everyone needs to be intentional about their healing because as I've just illustrated, you have no clue how you're negatively affecting your friends, family, children, co-workers, and even strangers. If you have a bad attitude, it's not because that's just who you are. You have a bad attitude because you're dwelling in hurt. Plain and simple. You haven't taken the time to acknowledge, understand, process, and resolve the hurt. The hurt just sits there and dwells in you and it creates bigger problems in your life. Understand too, at the end of the day, you're not just hurting other people, you're also hurting yourself.

Studies have shown that chronic stress has a significant negative effect on the immune system, ultimately manifesting in the body as terminal illness. Bottom line: stress contributes to diseases in your body. There is a direct link between stress and physical and mental illness.

When you're holding on to negativity and hurt, you're holding on to emotional stress as well. The reason stress is so dangerous is because you can't see it. Out of sight, out of mind. However, stress is real. It eats away at you in multiple ways, deteriorating your health. It's also important for me to point out that a lot of your struggles in life, stem from the hurt you've stored up over the years.

However, stress is also controllable and preventable. You can manage stress and you can heal from the triggers that create stress in your life. If every person on the planet does the work to heal and gets to a better place, we will eventually be able to break the hurt cycle currently plaguing our society. Before you know it, we'll have a much more positive, loving, wonderful community and world to live in.

Understand that if you've been hurt and you haven't healed, you've unconsciously been a part of the "hurt people, hurt people," cycle. Don't panic, it's okay. You didn't know any better. You don't need to beat yourself up about it. What's done is done. No need to dwell on or in the past. We're going to focus on how you're going to heal and make things better moving forward.

It's time to break the cycle.

You're Not Alone

When it comes to being hurt, it can feel like such an isolated and lonely place to be. It may seem like everyone else has it better than you. You may feel like nothing is worse than what you're going through or what you're feeling in the moment. It's very easy to become so consumed by your pain and disappointment that you can't see or even process the outside world. You get so stuck on being hurt, to the point you feel like no one else could possibly understand your pain. It may seem like you don't have anyone to lean on.

However, this is simply not true. Consciously or subconsciously what ends up happening is we push everyone away because when you've been hurt, you don't want to let anyone too close to you. Your heart is so fragile at this point, you feel the only solution is to isolate yourself.

Isolation is when you figuratively or literally crawl up in your little corner, feeling like you're going to die. The good news? You're not going to die. You're going to make it through this. You will overcome this and every other painful situation that comes your way in the future.

How do you start? You start by remembering you're not alone. As you read this, I want you to know, you're not the only person currently going through or who has been through heartbreak and pain. I'm not saying this to make you feel better. It's like when you're broke and people say, "Well, there are people in the world who have less than you." You know that. Hearing it doesn't make you feel better about being broke at the moment.

Understanding that other people are hurting too won't make your pain go away, but it can help you put things in perspective. It can keep you from going off the deep end when you really start to realize that this journey of pain and hurt doesn't need to be a lonely one.

There are people out here who understand you. There are people going through what you're going through right now, the exact same things. You are not alone. You should never feel alone.

I can't tell you how many times I've posted something on social media and when people begin to share their stories, other people respond, "Oh my gosh. I didn't realize someone else was going through the same thing too."

I would argue that much of the world is hurting. Realize that you are probably surrounded by hurt people all day, every day. Unfortunately, this is more common than not. Hurt has become our normal state of being. I don't want you to feel like you're the only person hurting while everyone else is all happy and in a good place.

People who are healed, they're the minority. You'll hear people say: "Well, everyone has issues." It's funny to me how we're quick to validate our issues and hold on to them for defense. However, we don't consider using this point of view when it comes to understanding what other people are going through and extending our hand with compassion.

Do I necessarily agree with this statement? No. Everyone doesn't still have issues. I would argue that everyone has had issues at one time or another. However, some people have already resolved their issues. They have taken the necessary steps and time out for healing, personal growth, and development. There are people among us that have gotten the help they needed and have done the work to be healthy, happy, whole individuals.

Not everyone has issues that are detrimental to their romantic relationships, friendships, family connections, businesses, and their ability to be successful in life. Not everyone has those types of issues.

Never use, "Everyone has issues," as validation to stay dwelling in yours. It's not a good excuse and it's not acceptable anymore. Being surrounded by other hurt people doesn't excuse you from ignoring your own need to heal from your hurt.

Listen, I love you. I want to see you win. I don't have to know you. I don't ever have to lay my eyes on you, however we're still somehow connected. I want the best for you. I want you to be happy and I want you to be healed. I mean that from the bottom of my heart.

I want you to know you have someone rooting for you.

Now, you may be reading this, and you may feel like you have no one. You may feel like you have no friends and there is really no one there for you. If this is you, please know you are loved. There is at least one person, me, on the planet who wants to see you win.

In addition to my love and support of you, you also need to know God loves you and God wants you in a better place. It's common to feel like even God has abandoned you in your moments of hurt and pain. You might question God's presence. Thinking, "Why has God allowed this to happen to me?"

Often, we turn our anger and resentment from our heartbreaks and other hurtful experiences toward God as well.

However, God is always present and always with you, no matter what you're going through or how you feel. The Bible says, "*Give all your worries and cares to God, for He cares about you.*" I Peter 5:7, NLT

I want you to know you are supported.

When we're hurting, we fail to realize or acknowledge the people who are in our lives, who deeply care for us. We don't allow ourselves to fully experience their love and support or fully grasp it, not because their love and support for us doesn't exist, but because we aren't allowing them to see our struggle. We're not being transparent and honest with them about the fact that we need help and a shoulder to cry on.

You might be putting on a persona, acting like you have it all together. That you're fine. That everything in your life is amazing. When that's not really what's going on. That's not how you're really feeling at all.

Behind closed doors you're a wreck. You're crying yourself to sleep at night. Behind closed doors, you're broken up and struggling. Again, this is nothing to be ashamed of. I'm not here to beat you up or make you feel worse. I'm here to bring to light what is true so you can properly address any unresolved issues once and for all.

For you to receive the help you need, the support you so desperately desire, you must be open and honest about your struggle. You can't hide behind the persona of, "I'm so strong, I've got it all together." You are still strong, even more so when you're going through. However, you're not required to have it all together, all the time. Ish happens. Period. It's nothing to be ashamed of.

Listen, we all have our moments. We're all human. This is life. This is just the way it is. Be more open and honest. Doing so will help you recognize the people who want to see you win. Transparency will allow you to see who has your back. It will allow you to see who you can connect with on a deeper level when you need them.

It's important to let people in. You need to be supported during times when you're hurting. However, it's equally important to discern who you can trust and who really loves you. Unfortunately, there are some people who will simply pour salt on your wound and make it more painful for you because of their own unresolved hurt. You must be mindful and wise about that.

Recognize the difference between the individual who doesn't know better and the individual who simply doesn't care about your feelings. Everyone has negative friends and family members who are so caught up in their own hurt and negativity, they simply don't care about how you feel. Even in this situation, the true root of their lack of empathy is not malicious. It's just that they're so consumed by their own feelings, they don't consider how their actions or words impact you.

These are the individuals, who mean well, but aren't always mindful of their delivery when giving you advice or showing their support. However, deep down, you know they love you and speak with good intentions. In this situation, the solution isn't to shut them out because now you're removing an ally from your team. You're removing someone who can be there, who can be a shoulder to cry on when you need it.

The key is to have an open, honest discussion with them about how their delivery impacts you. This way they'll be aware going forward and can make the appropriate corrections. Be mindful of the difference. Recognize the people who love you and want to see you win, but who don't always know how best to express it. Versus the individuals who don't want to see you win at all.

When you open yourself up and allow the right people to see your struggles, your test will become your testimony. If you've gone through painful and traumatic experiences, but have also reached a point of conquering those situations and healing from them, those things should be shared and celebrated.

When you're able to share your story without shame or guilt it can have a huge impact on other people's lives. That's the beautiful thing about healing and being transparent about what you've gone through. You're then equipped to help other people. You're able to set yourself free. The Bible says, *"And you will know the truth, and the truth will set you free."* John 8:32, NLT

It's so true. It's not just about hearing the truth, it's also about speaking your truth.

When you hold onto deep secrets and deep pain, closing everyone off, you remain in bondage to those things. It creates a struggle in your life. It's like a weight has been put around your neck, holding you down, keeping you from being fully free and moving in the direction you need to move. Forward.

When you expose your hurt and pain to the light and open up, allowing others to see the truth of who you are and what you've been through, and how you've overcome it, oh my goodness, so many people are going to be inspired. Even if it's not the masses, even if it's just the five people in your neighborhood, the three people in your family, or the same parents who hurt you. Knowing your struggles and your trials helps them break free from their own hurt and dysfunctional patterns.

Our healing is powerful enough to help other people break their cycles of pain, hurt, and disappointment. Sharing your story, your testimony, your truth, sets you and others free. That's the wonderful thing about the healing process. We really get to see on a greater scale that we're not alone, none of us are. No one's situation is so unique that someone else isn't going through it, hasn't gone through it, or will not go through it.

Someone needs to hear your story. Someone needs to hear your voice. You need to hear someone else's story. Together we're going to turn what was negative into a beautiful thread of collective healing. It's the positive cycle we can start to use to counter the negative one. When we begin to share ourselves with the people around us and with the world, it helps us heal and become more human to each other, more connected.

Again, begin to view the tests you face in life as power because they shape your testimony. Be open to facing, overcoming, and sharing your experiences with others. Realize there are other people who feel like they're alone too. When you come forth and share your experiences, you contribute to a community of people who can support each other, uplift each other, and get each other to a higher level in life.

Choose to create beauty among the ruins. When we share our stories, it helps us to know we're not alone in life. Speak up to connect with others when you're going through the trials of life. You'll be strengthened and so will others.

The Bible encourages us in Revelation 12:11, *"And they have defeated him by the blood of the Lamb and by the power of their testimony."*

Your testimony is your power.

PART II

THE
Release
PROCESSING YOUR PAIN &
HURTFUL EXPERIENCES

PUT THE HURT OUT
IN FRONT OF YOU

A good portion of our lives is spent running from our issues. Escapism is a part of our DNA. Why do you think movie stars, Hollywood, athletes, and television networks make so much money? They're all in charge of keeping us distracted from the unpleasant realities of life. We live our lives trying to ignore our issues and trying to convince ourselves we're good. We lie to ourselves and others, by repeating "I'm fine." Trying to convince yourself that you don't have any problems. Pretending "it" isn't affecting you anymore or that the unresolved issues are no longer issues in your life is a waste of time and energy.

The reality is it's simply not true. Of course, you can tell yourself whatever you want to hear. You can also try to convince everyone else around you of your untruth. However, your behavior, your energy, your mindset, all these things will tell a different, deeper story. They will betray your words and show others that something *is* going on within you.

We have become conditioned to believe that the ways we tend to act out life is just an extension of who we are. It's almost like when people say, "Well, I'm just not an affectionate person. I didn't experience a lot of affection growing up. It's just not who I am."

First, not being affectionate has nothing to do with who you are. It's who you became. It's who you were programmed to be and became due to your experiences. Let's go deeper. I believe there's no such thing as "you're not an affectionate person." I believe you may struggle with the emotions associated with showing affection. You may struggle with giving or receiving affection and there is a deeper reason for this.

We need to stop just looking at the surface of our issues. Understand that almost everything has a deeper explanation. So, for the person who says they aren't affectionate, they can be around children and become ultra-affectionate. They'll have no problem opening-up, showing love, and being touchy-feely.

Then put them around an adult or someone of the opposite sex and now it's like, "Don't touch me." They become very guarded.

This example has nothing to do with a lack of affection present in the person. The reason they can show affection to the child is because the child doesn't pose a threat to their feelings. In that situation, the person is much more willing to be vulnerable and open, easily able to show outward affection. Whereas with the adult, the person becomes guarded because of negative conditioning, which has taught them the adult could hurt them. They don't allow themselves to be vulnerable, which interprets their ability to show affection in the situation.

Again, lack of showing affection speaks to a deeper issue. Everything boils down to the fact that there is something going on within you keeping you from being who you truly are.

Let's start to identify the deeper things holding you back and start to pull them out. It's important for you to put the hurt out in front of you. That's what this chapter is all about. You're no longer going to just make excuses or convince yourself you aren't struggling in some areas and that no problems exist.

No. Let's really go deep now and pinpoint things. So far, we've been discussing a lot of different signs, behaviors, and angles of identifying unresolved hurt to help you warm up to this process. Now it's time for you to begin taking steps toward your healing.

THE WHO HURT ME LIST

The first step of my healing method is called the "Who Hurt Me List." If you purchased the companion workbook, you can turn to the section corresponding with this chapter. If you don't have the companion workbook, grab your dedicated notebook and something to write with. I highly recommend purchasing the companion workbook to keep all your healing exercises in one place and to get additional resources to help you on your healing journey. Whatever you use, make sure you're only using it to complete the healing exercises.

If you're working in your own notebook, at the top of the first page write: "Who hurt me?" Take a moment and ask yourself this question out loud. Allow yourself a little quiet time to listen for the answers. Certain people will begin to come to mind for you. Whoever comes to mind, write their name down. I don't care if you think the person or situation is no longer relevant and you think you've moved past things, whoever comes to mind, write their name and the experience associated with them down. The fact that they came to mind means they're significant in some way.

On the next page you will find an example of a previous client's "Who Hurt Me" list, which I was given permission to use to help you get started. Of course, each person's life experience is going to be different. However, I feel the example will help prompt your own memories and help you get the ball rolling on completing your list.

"WHO HURT ME" LIST SAMPLE

(Example list used with client's permission.)

1. God
   a. For allowing me to grow up in such a toxic, unloving environment as a child
   b. For allowing the enemy to do everything possible to kill off my ability to love
   c. For allowing me to experience every possible misfortunate life experience every four years
   d. For me getting raped, molested, abandoned, emotionally and verbally abused as a child
   e. For being born in a family full of dysfunction and pain

2. Mom
   a. For your over critical nature that always made me feel like I wasn't good enough
   b. For your lack of affection and expressed love my entire life
   c. For you valuing things and wanting to buy me and the bad example that love can be bought

3. Dad
   a. For not caring enough to make sure you played an active role in my life as a child
   b. For deciding not to be around in my adult life either
   c. For your selfishness and inherited generational issues

4. Sister Carla
   a. For your lack of restraint when it came to your drinking and violent treatment toward your family members
   b. For treating me poorly as a teenager and wanting to buy and control me

    c.   For leaving me alone in a hostile environment once you finished high school

    d.   For not forgiving yourself and me when I got raped

    e.   For you blaming yourself as if it were within your control and for treating me with resentment because of your guilt

5. Grandmother

    a.   For picking a man over everything else

    b.   For being a shitty mother and creating brokenness and abandonment in our bloodline

    c.   For your lack of courage where your relationships were concerned

    d.   For not believing me about your youngest son molesting me

    e.   For being a poor example of how to live life as a woman

6. Brad- lover

    a.   For not communicating with me honestly about our household finances and your needing help with the bills

    b.   For allowing yourself to be consumed with possessiveness & jealousy and treating me poorly as a result

    c.   For breaking my heart

    d.   For shattering my trust and not fighting for our relationship

    e.   For not being confident in my love for you

    f.   For not working on yourself & building up your confidence and self-esteem & resenting me for having my shit together as a result

Unlike the client who allowed me to use her list for this book, I once had a client who was the exact opposite of cooperative with facing her past. We'll call her Carla. She was a young woman in her late twenties. I could clearly see at our first in-person session, she was holding on to a lot of unresolved hurt and pain. It was visible. I could literally see it on her. I could see it in her energy. It was audible in how she spoke about certain things. It was very clear to me she was only giving off the impression she had it all together, completely unaware that her efforts were in vain.

I'll let you know a little-known secret about me, I've been given a gift where I can just look at someone and read between the lines. I can see past whatever façade they're trying to present to the world, and I can tell if something is wrong.

In addition to my gift, I also pay close attention to a person's energy. Their energy will tell me the truth about their state of being. Their spirit will alert me to any problem(s) present. So, it was very clear from the first time I met Carla there were some deeply rooted issues present within her.

When Carla and I started to finally discuss things, I instructed her to do the "Who Hurt Me List" exercise. A week later, at our next session, she tells me, "I did the exercise, but no one came to mind."

My first thought was: "This is some bull."

My actual response was: "Wait a minute, there's no way your list is blank and not a single person came to mind. You mean to tell me no one has ever hurt you?"

First, I don't know if there are any adults on this planet who've never been hurt by anyone or anything. You can't possibly convince me of that. Not to mention it was obvious to me Carla was in pain and hurting, even though she was trying her best to not outwardly show it.

I continued to explain my position. "Majority of people don't properly heal from their hurt. So, chances are, you not only have experienced some hurt from your past experiences, you also have some unresolved hurt dwelling within you. So, to tell me no one came to mind for the "Who Hurt Me List" exercise shows me you're suppressing your feelings.

To be completely honest with you, I think you're a mastermind manipulator."

What's a mastermind manipulator? Someone who is an expert at convincing themselves of whatever they need to believe to not deal with certain things. This allows them to be able to move forward in a way they're comfortable with, but not in a way that's healthy.

Carla had convinced herself she was A-Okay. She truly believed there was nothing wrong. However, it was lies. I knew it. She knew it. However, she'd completely bought into the lie. So much so, she couldn't possibly risk having to admit it. I understood completely.

It's scary to have to confront your pain and to address your issues.

This is one of the reasons why I want you to fully complete this exercise. Because we fear facing ourselves, our hurt, and our past, we run. We've been running from things for so long it's become a part of our natural behavior. Since we haven't properly addressed our issues, things have piled up. Now, we feel like it's too hard to properly process and organize our thoughts because it feels so overwhelming. It's easier to keep running or to just shut down completely.

However, you're reading this book because it's finally time to stop running and to face things once and for all. No more suppressing your feelings. No more trying to convince yourself, nothing's wrong, when there is.

When doing this exercise. Truly let yourself go there. Do not hold back with this list. You need this release and complete healing like you need air to breathe. Allow yourself to open up. Chances are you've got a lot bottled up that needs to be released. Don't be surprised by what comes out when you really go deep within and ask yourself the question, "who hurt me?"

You don't need to share this list with anyone or the things that come up when working through this personal process.

I honestly recommend doing it alone and taking your time. Be patient with yourself. Be kind, gentle, and loving with yourself. This exercise will trigger a strong emotional response. That's normal. It's healthy. Granted, it's not what we want. Honestly, it's exactly what we've been trying to avoid. However, it's for your overall good.

Once you have your "Who Hurt Me List" completed, you'll need to begin to pinpoint your pain. It's very difficult to process through your emotions and get to the bottom of your source of hurt—which is the place where you really need to begin to heal—if everything is kind of just all jumbled up in your head.

Keeping everything in a state of blurred vagueness has probably served as a coping mechanism of some kind. You've stored your pain in a proverbial dark closet all this time. You've gotten in the habit of throwing every hurtful experience in there as fast as it happens. This has been a feeble attempt to forget about it. What happens over time is you trick yourself into thinking you've gotten over things, but you haven't properly resolved anything, you've only moved past things on the surface.

You may have moved forward in life. You may not think about the hurtful experiences daily. You may not see on the surface how it impacts you, but that doesn't mean it's not eating at your ability to love and show love in relationships with yourself and others. If you haven't properly identified the hurt and the other people involved, acknowledged how it made you feel, allowed yourself to feel those feelings, instead of brushing them off, and forgiven yourself and them, you haven't properly resolved anything.

You haven't really healed.

The pain is still there. It's still lingering in the shadows. You're just not acknowledging it. You're essentially doing what I call stuffing it into your emotional closet.

When you experience hurtful things, you stuff them into your closet, lock the door, and walk away. You think you're good, but you're not. Then if something else happens, you go back, you open the door, you stuff the new thing into the closet, lock the door, and walk away. Again, you think you're good.

Essentially, you're in denial. Until one day you're going to go to store something else in your emotional/denial closet and everything is going to come pouring out. It can only hold so much. You can only hold so much in.

The result of the excess buildup once the closet is at capacity is a huge mess. Everything you put in there that you didn't want to deal with as it happened, pours over you all at once. You in turn are a huge mess, a wreck. It's going to hit you harder than it's ever hit you before because out of sight, out of mind, works until you must face everything all at once.

A lot of times when people have a breakdown or are going through an intense emotional experience, it's not just the result of one isolated incident. It's a combination of all the past hurts and pain that have now reached the full capacity of containment. Everything is now magnified because none of it was addressed.

Properly addressing past issues, makes you better equipped to handle your current issues. The reality is you're always going to be facing something. It's a part of life. Again, the difference is if you resolve things as they happen, you'll have the energy to resolve new issues as they come up. You'll have a better mindset on how to handle yourself and your emotions. You'll also have more knowledge, understanding, and wisdom on how to overcome things and they won't seem as difficult to tackle.

However, when you allow hurt and pain to linger, it will eventually hit you like a ton of bricks. It's going to be one of the hardest things you'll ever deal with. Let's not add anything else to the closet and instead of being caught off guard, let's address and resolve the issues now to keep them from continuing to pile up.

Completing the "Who Hurt Me List" allows you to see and pinpoint your unresolved pain. You'll be able to recognize where some of your negative energy comes from. It could be your parents. It could be pain from past romantic relationships, friendships, co-workers, it could be anything.

I mean, listen, as human beings, we can act like we don't care about this, that, and the other, but a lot of times, we do care. What someone else says or does in some way or another will impact you. It can impact your perception of yourself. It can impact your confidence and how you move forward in certain areas of your life.

Getting your hurt out in front of you and seeing it for what it is, is going to be a very enlightening experience. You'll have something tangible to look at. You'll be able to clearly see what you've been holding on to. You'll be able to look at what's been lingering inside you. This is the other reason why I'm having you do this exercise. I want you to face the pain once and for all. I don't want you to run from it anymore. By doing this list, you're ultimately saying, "no more running." You won't be able to run anymore or live in denial.

At the end of the day, when you don't take time to figure out the cause of your hurt and pain and to acknowledge it, you're more likely to continue to ignore it. You give yourself permission to continue to act like it doesn't exist. You allow yourself to be distracted by life in a way that you don't ever have to truly face your pain.

Now, listen, there may be instances that in certain situations you have genuinely healed from things. I'm not saying you're still carrying every single hurtful experience from your past inside of you. There are probably situations you have dealt with previously and healed from.

However, I would still like you to write down the name of anyone that comes to mind while doing the 'Who Hurt Me List' exercise. I've found that sometimes people have tried certain healing methods like traditional therapy or alternative medicine for emotional issues and for whatever reason they weren't able to get the healing they needed from these methods.

It doesn't mean there was anything wrong with the methods, it means that for whatever reason, the result wasn't complete healing from your issues. In other situations, a person might think since they've been able to go on with their life, it means they've healed. However, in most cases no healing has taken place at all. They've just learned to suppress their issue(s). Suppressing their issues may have made the person feel good temporarily. They may have been able to cope and manage the situation better, but true healing never occurred.

Also, in some circumstances, there may be certain aspects of a situation you've healed from, but not the entire situation. As you actively participate in the exercises included in the *Stephan Speaks Healing Method* it will ensure you experience complete healing.

Again, if someone pops up in your head and you say to yourself, "Wait a minute, I dealt with that. I went to a therapist. I did this, or I did that, so maybe I shouldn't put them on the list." Put them on the list anyway. We need to explore why they're still popping up. Why they're still coming to mind?

Listen, if when we continue through the process and it turns out you really, truly have gotten it all out of your system and you're good and it's been addressed, all right, cool. You'll get to erase them afterwards.

However, they need to be included to make sure. We don't want anything lingering. Once each issue is resolved, you can cross the person off the list, but not until you've completed the entire process per person and related experience.

The last thing I want is for you to read this book, go through the process, truly commit to it, and then you're still broken or still hurting afterward. Then it would all be pointless.

My goal here is to make sure you get the healing you need. That's why I really want you to fully embrace everything you need to do. Don't skip any of the steps. Don't make excuses or find ways to get around doing your part to make sure you're completely healed at the end of this journey.

Putting the hurt out in front of you, being able to see it, acknowledging it, is just the first step. However, it is a vital first step in your experiencing complete healing.

ET THINGS OFF
YOUR CHEST

Part I
SPEAKING YOUR TRUTH

"You heal by releasing, not suppressing." This quote speaks true to what we've discussed so far and what we're about to explore in more depth in this chapter.

As we've already discussed, holding on to past hurt creates a lot of issues in your life. The impact unresolved hurt has on you can be both conscious and subconscious. Many ailments and illnesses that show up physically in the body, can be traced back to a lack of emotional health.

Everything is connected.

Let me give you an example. I once knew a woman in her late 30s. She was a very accomplished military officer. We'll call her Catherine. Catherine took great care of herself physically. She had a nice shape. She also took time to learn about proper nutrition and eating right. However, she ended up being diagnosed with cancer. To those who knew her, it just didn't make any sense.

"How could someone who took so great care of themselves be diagnosed with cancer?" Everyone questioned.

I acknowledge that I'm not a medical professional or any type of authority on cancer and there are all kinds of possible contributing factors to explain how Catherine still developed cancer. The fact is cancer can develop in your body, despite how well you eat, or how good of shape you're in.

However, it's also been scientifically proven that when you're taking proper care of yourself from a physical standpoint you can decrease the chances of developing cancer significantly.

Back to Catherine and my example. Despite how well she took care of her physical health, she was letting the unseen affect her overall health. Everything appeared to be well put together on the surface, however, beneath the surface, she was an emotional wreck.

She was in a very toxic relationship, which had turned abusive. She was very unhappy with her relationship and her unhappiness spilled over into every other area of her life.

A dysfunctional relationship has the power to negatively affect every other area of your life.

No matter how much she smiled and tried to put on a good front, no matter how much she tried to act like everything was all good, those unresolved issues including her toxic relationship ended up cancelling out her healthy physical lifestyle.

Let me tell you, when you're in a toxic relationship, your issues didn't just start in the toxic relationship. The fact that you allowed yourself to even get into this relationship and are still there is proof there's almost a 100% chance an unresolved issue existed before the relationship started. It's the reason why you've entered this type of relationship in the first place.

I truly believe Catherine's cancer developed as a result of the emotional stress she was carrying by not letting things out, by suppressing so much, and not properly dealing with her emotional issues. This example might seem to side on the extreme, but I can't stress to you enough, why it's so important you get things off your chest and start to release. It's literally a matter of life or death.

If you want to heal and be healthier in every aspect of your being, you've got to clean yourself out and remove the things that are either currently making you sick or can contribute to future illness. What we're going to do next is essentially an emotional detox.

Just like if you wanted to bring yourself to greater health from a physical standpoint, you would need to detox first. You could start eating healthier tomorrow and doing all the wonderful things nutritionists say will have a positive impact, but for your body to be able to reap the benefits of your healthier changes, you first need to get rid of all the waste. You would need to get your body to a place where it can receive the nutrients of the good food, you're now going to put in it.

It's the same thing from an emotional standpoint. You can pile on a great job, a nice house, and what seems to be a great relationship. I say "seems" because there are so many people fronting and acting like the relationship is great when it's not or the relationship seems great at first, but that's only because you're ignoring all the red flags. It's actually a disaster waiting to happen. I digress. You can pile all these wonderful things up, but guess what? You're still not going to be happy. You're still not going to be good at your core because you haven't cleaned yourself out emotionally.

You must go through a process of getting unresolved things off your chest and flushing out the backed up negative energy. So, how do you accomplish this?

I mentioned this earlier and I will mention it again. *"And you will know the truth, and the truth will set you free."* John 8:32, NLT

It's not just about hearing the truth. It's about speaking your truth.

When you suppress negative emotions and energy and aren't open and honest about your true feelings, you're basically in bondage to lies and deceit. You put up a façade instead of being honest about what's really going on. You try to act like everything is all good, but, truthfully, you're in jail to your emotions, hurts, and fears. All these things are paralyzing you. They're keeping you from moving forward and living your best life.

In order to free yourself, as the scripture says, you must speak your truth. You need to release your truth into the atmosphere. Let it come out of you. This is how you're going to continue the path of healing. Speaking your truth allows you to acknowledge your real issues. When you acknowledge your real issues, you can face them. Once you're able to face them, you'll be able to conquer them, learn from them, and become better from them.

You can't fix something you won't acknowledge exists. You can't overcome an obstacle if you keep telling yourself there are no obstacles. Be honest with yourself during this process.

It can be very hard to conquer your issues and see things clearly when you're in the situation because your emotions are involved. Emotions make it very difficult to properly evaluate things. That's why some people who are great at giving advice are horrible at taking their own advice. It's not because they don't have good advice or accurate answers, it's just that once emotions are involved and they're emotionally invested in a situation, it screws up their perception. It makes it more difficult to see things for what they are.

A great way to go about speaking your truth is seeing a helping professional. Going to talk to a helping professional is always a great thing to do because it can help you get a better understanding of what's going on inside of you, your behaviors, and life as a result. It also helps you to release and speak your truth without judgement. It's good to have someone on the outside of your situation looking in to help you see things properly. Going to a therapist or having a coach is always advised. It's a great thing to invest in.

THE BENEFITS OF SEEING A HELPING PROFESSIONAL

Helping professionals include therapists, life and relationship coaches, guidance counselors, social workers, pastors, or other spiritual leaders. Below are a few reasons why you would benefit from seeking out a professional third party to work through your healing.

UNBIASED PERSPECTIVE

If you go to a friend, a family member, or anyone who has any attachment or involvement in the situation, they may not be capable of giving you good, sound advice. It's very easy for them to be biased. Maybe they secretly want to see things work out or they secretly want to see you leave the person. Maybe your friend or family member is going through the same exact situation, a tough marriage or a difficult relationship. If they're not able to leave their situation for whatever reason, they'll have a very hard time encouraging you to leave yours, if that's what you need to do.

With a helping professional there is no bias. There is no emotional attachment to what's going on in your situation. They can give a more objective opinion on action steps you can take to improve your situation and the outcome.

A helping professional has probably worked with others going through the same type of situation you're facing. They understand the dynamics better than the average person and have more insight on how to properly handle the situation and help you work through it. They've seen what strategies will and won't work for certain situations you may be facing.

NO JUDGEMENT ZONE

A helping professional isn't going to judge you or your situation. Our job is not to judge you. It's to listen. To help you release. To be an ear and to help you see things more clearly. The absence of judgement makes it easier for you to open up, to be more vulnerable and truthful about how you feel, and what's going on in your situation.

WHAT TO LOOK FOR IN A HELPING PROFESSIONAL

1. Look for someone who specializes in dealing with your particular issue.

> ▶ For example, if you're dealing with sexual abuse issues, it's good to look for a helping professional who has experience helping survivors of sexual abuse.

▸ If you're dealing with relationship problems, it's better for you to seek a relationship coach vs. going to a general life coach. Choose someone who specializes in the area you need help in.

2. Find someone you generally feel comfortable with. There's no point in going to someone you don't feel comfortable being around. It's not going to be a good fit if something about them bothers you or you feel like you don't trust them. You need someone who makes you feel at ease and who you are peaceful about being yourself around.

3. Look for someone who is going to encourage you to take the necessary steps to make changes to help improve your overall situation and life. Remember this is about you getting healed and being healthy, mind, body, spirit. You want someone who is going to partner with you to begin to take steps toward an overall better you.

When possible, I recommend seeking out a helping professional who will partner with you to work through your healing. Now, I know some people are against the thought of therapy and counseling. I'm not here to argue with you on your position one way or another. I just want to make sure I give you all the tools available for your use.

However, I also understand not everyone will have the capability or finances to seek professional help. This is one of the main reasons I wrote this book. I truly believe it will help you overcome the limitations or barriers keeping you in your hurt and brokenness with or without a helping professional. This book serves as a silent third party because I want everyone to have access to the steps they can take to self-heal.

Whether or not you have access to a helping professional, another way to speak your truth and heal is to release your story into the air. If you live by a lake or the ocean or have a favorite spot you go to for peace and serenity —this could be your car, a walk-in closet, etc.—go there and just talk out your feelings. Release your pain and issues on to the wind and let the wind carry them far from your heart.

In addition to this spoken release and flushing this negative energy out of your system verbally, you're also going to write letters to the people on the "Who Hurt Me List."

Part II
LETTER WRITING RELEASE

You've probably heard of the benefits of letter writing before for healing purposes. However, let me be clear, even if you've done a similar process in the past, there's a very specific approach I need you to do regarding writing the letter(s) now. It might be different from how you've tried it before. For this reason, even if you've done this exercise already, I want you to be open to doing it again. If you've done a similar exercise before and you're still struggling in certain areas with the same people coming to mind during the 'Who Hurt Me List' exercise, it means the issue wasn't properly addressed with the previous version of the letter. Maybe you didn't get everything out of your system.

I am extremely confident that if you write the letter again during this process, you're going to finally get the issue resolved.

There will be two drafts of each letter you need to write.

WRITING THE FIRST DRAFT

The first draft is arguably the most important of the two drafts. In the first draft, you're going to let it all hang out. What do I mean? There is no holding back.

Pick someone from your "Who Hurt Me List." Let's say your mother made your list, your first letter would be addressed to your mother. You'd begin by writing her a letter that is honest about your feelings toward her and the experiences she's caused that have hurt you. See an example of a rough draft letter written to the mother of a client below.

MOM LETTER EXAMPLE: FIRST DRAFT-RAW EDITION
(Example list used with client's permission.)

Dear Mom,

I think you're a selfish, self-centered, naïve, airhead. I understand now what I didn't understand when I was a child. You lack the gift of common sense and are incredibly narrow-minded. You get stuck on ideals that aren't attainable and you love playing the fucking victim. You never take ownership of the shit that you're the cause of. I don't hate you, but I strongly dislike the person that I now have the opportunity to see with adult eyes.

I think you're weak and pathetic. I've witnessed you put the false love of a man over your children and yourself. I had to actively work to make sure I didn't follow in the footsteps that you and your mother gave by letting men abuse you both—physically, emotionally, and verbally—take everything good, and leave you both drained and broken just for the sake of you all not wanting to be alone.

This showed me what it looks like when you don't like or love yourself. Your lack of self-love was passed down to me and my siblings. Your brokenness, your issues, everything. I only had examples of what not to do. No practical examples of how to be healthy and loving toward myself. As a mother, why didn't you ever consider your children in your decision making, since we were directly affected by everything you did or didn't do?

I'm pissed at the fact that you had children who are now adults and are fucked up, using drugs and alcohol to cope, swimming in cyclical poverty and depression, based off decisions that you made that we had no control over. I'm pissed off because you were supposed to fucking know better. We're trying to function as adults, heal, and figure it out now, but it's hard as hell when you feel like you never had a chance. We weren't even given a proper start. Just targets on our backs and statistics to define our fate. Paying for your and our mistakes. It's a fucking lot to deal with and I'm sick of fucking pretending with you.

As a result of your not being there, I developed abandonment issues, I lacked self-esteem, I dealt with unworthiness issues. Looking for love in other people who only wanted to use me up and make me something common and unvalued. I have struggled with feeling like I needed to be perfect in order to be shown love, which resulted in me being overcritical of myself, at times, to the point of crippling my life and my ability to move forward in my relationships. I adopted a self-defeating attitude of never being satisfied or liking myself.

How can I possibly love myself if I can't find anything I like about me? For a long time I could only see my flaws and shortcomings and nothing good, nothing beautiful. I felt void of beauty and desire. I felt ugly and unlovable. The "family" that was supposed to protect me was the cause of majority of my early insecurities. Never having anything positive to pour into me, only negativity, toxic-energy, and misery because they were miserable.

I have struggled with silent, functional depression almost my whole life. I have endured unspeakable hurt and pain at the hands of others because of the voids that come from a broken dysfunctional childhood upbringing and household.

You fucked up. Plain and simple. You fucked up mom. Big time.

In the first draft of your letters, you're going to be brutally honest about how you feel. You might need to curse your mother out. Something you probably wouldn't dare do in real life. This is your chance to be uncensored and true to your feelings. It's time to let it all out. Don't hold back. Don't try to be politically correct. Don't try to dance around any issues. Release. Get all the raw emotion out. You need this moment of true release, of not filtering your raw emotions. This is the purpose of writing the first draft.

Allow your emotions to flow. This is a part of your core healing. Allow yourself to cry if needed. Crying is a healthy form of release. It's okay to cry. We all hurt. We've all been there, man or woman it makes no difference. Again, don't hold any emotion back. If you find yourself getting extremely angry, allow yourself to get angry. Allow yourself to go through every raw emotion that comes to the surface during this exercise because again, you need to purge them from your system.

This is the start of your emotional detox. If you've done a detox before of any kind, a lot of times when we're cleaning ourselves out, all the bad stuff starts to come out first. So, going through the negative emotions of extreme hurt and pain is normal. That's the process. Allow yourself to process through the bad in order to get to the good, which eventually leads to the great. Although it might not feel good at first, don't fight it, don't censor anything, just let it all pour out.

As you go through this process, remember, commit to doing whatever it takes to fully release. If it means your letter requires you to write 30 or 40 pages, do it. That may sound like an exaggeration, but it may not be. You may have a ridiculous number of things you've been holding on to that you've never fully expressed.

Again, if you need to take 30 or 40 pages to fully express yourself, take them. It doesn't matter how long the letter is. The goal is to get everything out of you that's been stuck.

On the other hand, if you genuinely only have one-page worth of release, that's cool too. All I care about is that you truly allow everything to come out of you and you don't hold anything back. Since this process is going to be very emotionally taxing, you may need to complete the letter writing exercise in stages. You may need to take breaks in between each person/ experience when doing this. That's perfectly fine.

Pace yourself.

I honestly don't expect you to be able to knock this out in one night or one day. You may start today and depending on what you have going on in your life, kids, work, a business, you might not have a full day to devote to sitting down and writing. I get it. However, schedule time for yourself to get this done and take breaks as necessary.

However, I don't want you to shelve this for too long. I don't want you to put it off indefinitely or even worse, not begin at all, using lack of time as an excuse. I also don't want you to start and then step away from it because it gets too tough and not come back to it until next year or even worse, never.

Make the choice to get healthy. Make time. Be consistent until each letter is complete.

A good way to write the letters is at the very least to add to the letter daily, almost like a diary or journal. Keep going back to it so that you keep the ball rolling and you're allowing everything to flow out. The more time you take in between writing a complete letter, the more of a struggle it might be to continue writing it. You may feel like, "Man, that was rough. I don't want to go back there." However, you've got to. You need to.

The healing process isn't easy. However, I promise you it's going to be beneficial when it's all said and done. Again, don't get discouraged at how many pages it takes you to experience a full release. Start each letter to the people on your 'Who Hurt Me' list and then keep it going. Don't stop until you get everything out of your system and address every issue you need to face.

Also, I highly encourage you to pray and meditate during your entire healing process, but especially during the letter writing release process. Prayer and meditation will help get you to a calm place in order to clear your mind. Prayer will also keep you encouraged and strengthened throughout this process.

Once you're done writing your first drafts, you're going to feel a lot better. You're going to feel like a weight has been lifted off your shoulders. The initial release you experience from writing the first drafts alone is very important and very meaningful in and of itself.

However, it's not enough to stop there. Just because you feel better, doesn't mean you're done with the process and have healed completely from each experience. I want to make sure you not only feel better in the moment, but that you eliminate and heal from all your past issues for good. I don't want them to keep coming back up and causing you to remain in negative cycles in your life that harbor negative outcomes in your relationships.

Once the first drafts of your letters are complete allow them to rest for one or two days. Again, use this time to pray and meditate to calm yourself and get peace about the release.

A simple prayer to pray is: "Father forgive us for we know not what we do." This prayer helps you to further release unforgiveness. It also allows you to include yourself in the prayer for the times you might've hurt yourself or others unknowingly. It's a good place to humble yourself before God. Give your offenses and offenders to Him. He will handle them so you can be free.

After the rest period is over, read the letter(s) to yourself as if you were the person you wrote it to. You're going to put yourself in their shoes for the moment.

As you read, pay attention to any language that comes off as attacking, condescending, or blatantly hurtful and insulting. It would be a good idea to grab a different color pen or a sticky note pad so you can mark up your first draft. These are things you're going to clean up in the second draft. Take the necessary time to process your thoughts and feelings to be sure you're communicating with clarity and love.

WRITING THE SECOND DRAFT

The harder part of the two drafts is over. Take a deep breath and do something to celebrate yourself, your courage, and your commitment to healing. You've released your pinned-up, raw emotions, processed and prayed over them, now you're ready to write the second draft of your letter(s).

Look at the first draft of a letter you wrote and the notes you wrote to yourself after reading it as the receiver. Again, pay close attention to the things you said in your raw emotional state that might be offensive, hurtful, or insulting. It's now time to rewrite your letter.

Let me be clear here. You're not changing your message, you're just changing the delivery of your message. The goal by the end of the second draft is to have fully expressed yourself and your truth in a more calm and loving manner.

Calm and loving doesn't mean you aren't going to express some hard truths in your letter. It doesn't mean some of the things you reveal and express aren't going to be a punch to the gut for the person if they were to read it. I say "if" because you may or may not be able to send the letter or have reasons why it wouldn't be a good idea to send it. However, we'll tackle the letter sending part of the process later. Let's not jump ahead.

Understand, there's a huge difference between lashing out at someone and expressing how someone made you feel. Your main goal with the letter is to clearly express the impact of the person's actions on/in your life. You want to make sure clarity is the tone of the second draft of the letter.

Another reason why the second draft of your letter is important is because if you're going to send the letter, it's important to learn how to express yourself clearly and in a positive and loving manner. This process isn't just for the sake of healing in this moment. This process is setting you up to better handle your relationships and future issues going forward.

One of the problems many people have is not knowing how to take their negative feelings and emotions and express themselves in a way that's effective. You see, communication is pointless if your communication consists of lashing out, attacking the other person, or speaking down to them. All this does is cause them to go into defense mode and nothing is accomplished once both of you are on the attack.

Going into defense mode is human nature. Anytime someone feels attacked, yourself included, they're going to defend themselves. There has probably been a moment in your life where you may have done something wrong. You knew you were wrong, but the way someone came at you regarding it, made you still defend yourself. Had they simply come at you in a more positive, calm, loving manner, and not in attack mode, you would've been more likely to let your walls down and been willing to own up and take accountability for your actions.

Now, I'm not saying it'll be automatic for the person to take accountability and accept what they've done wrong simply because you've expressed yourself more effectively. However, you do increase the chances of them receiving the message you want to convey to them when you communicate without attacking them. Whether you're dating, single, in a relationship, dealing with family problems, whatever the case may be, you want to learn how to effectively express yourself.

The more you practice this, the better you'll get at it, and the more effective it will be in your relationships and every other aspect of your life.

When you learn how to clearly and effectively express yourself to people—remember, it's not what you say, but how you say it—then you can get so much more out of every relationship in your life. This applies to romantic relationships, friendships, family ties, career relationships, and so on.

Remember we're working together to break the "hurt people, hurt people" cycle. The goal of your final letter isn't to attack the person with negativity or talk down to them. Your first draft gave you a chance to fully release all your anger onto the page. The first drat was for you, not them, which is why that's not the letter you're going to send.

You might ask, "Well, why can't I just speak to them and express how I feel verbally about the situation? Why can't we just have a conversation and I let them know how I feel?"

That's a good question. The reality is when you express your true emotions and deeper issues are involved, verbal conversations, 99% of the time aren't going to go well. Having a conversation with the person is usually not going to accomplish what you set out to accomplish.

People get defensive very quickly. They deflect. There is a higher risk of distractions during a verbal conversation on both sides. You may lose your train of thought and not fully articulate yourself or express all your feelings to the person. The person may choose to cut the conversation short. There is just so much that can go wrong with a verbal conversation.

The reason I recommend you communicate your feelings in a letter is because a letter gives you an opportunity to truly process your feelings, to truly get everything out, to not hold things back, without having the pressure of the moment. Let's face it, when we're sitting and talking to someone and we're expressing some heavy things, we can get scared. We can get nervous. We can get sidetracked and simply forget the point we wanted to make. Even if the person is receptive to what we're saying, there is always the possibility it can go left.

I'm not going to sit here and say that no one has ever had a successful verbal conversation for the purpose of getting things off their chest for their healing. However, it's just extremely risky and highly unlikely to go as planned. It's not likely to have a successful outcome.

Writing a letter has a higher chance of being effective for the purposes of achieving your healing and having a favorable outcome on both sides.

There is one exception to this rule. I have learned that some people struggle with writing, plain and simple. It can be hard to sit down and put your thoughts down on paper. Some people, myself included, are better speakers than writers. It's much easier for us to speak our minds than to write out our thoughts and feelings. If you're one of these people, I suggest recording yourself instead.

Complete the first draft of your letter by recording your thoughts instead of writing them down. Thanks to modern technology, you don't even need to go out and buy a recorder. You can download an app to your smartphone for free and complete your recording this way.

The initial recording would count as your first draft. The same rules apply here. Let it all out in your voice recording just like you would if you were writing it down on paper. I want you to be honest and allow yourself to process through the emotions that need to be felt and released.

However, once you get to your second draft, I strongly recommend you write it out in letter format. Listen to the recording again and begin to identify the parts that need to be edited out for the second draft. Then, all you're doing is putting your spoken words down on paper. Once you map out how to clean up your recording and express yourself in a positive and loving manner, you'll be good to go.

Let me just say, I'm not completely against doing a second draft by recording and sending it, but I honestly think a letter would be more effective. Hands down, my experience has been that the letter is the most effective method to use when going through this process and experiencing healing.

Part III
SENDING THE LETTERS

The next step in getting things off your chest is sending the letters to the recipients. However, before you do anything, it's important for you to pray and ask God if you should send the letter to the person.

I'm typically a strong supporter of sending the letter. However, I acknowledge that there are different dynamics at play depending on the situation. Here are my general guidelines on when I believe sending the letter is a must and where I think you have some flexibility as far as not sending it.

WHEN TO SEND THE LETTER

If the individual is someone you communicate with, even if it's not daily or weekly, but you still interact with this individual, I believe they need to receive the letter.

As I said earlier in the book, people who have hurt you don't always know and understand how they've negatively impacted your life. As much as you may think, well, "they should know," or "they should've known better," that's not always the case. I can argue, it's usually not the case. They often have no idea how their actions, words, or behaviors have negatively impacted your life. They probably don't know how hurt you are or have any clue you're holding on to any anger, resentment, or pain towards them. Sending the letter and allowing them to read it is going to help bring awareness to the situation. It's also going to decrease the chances of them triggering you going forward.

For example, if you've written a letter to your mother about a certain thing, she does that gets under your skin, the letter should help. If you fully express yourself in your letter and communicate clearly, she will now be aware of the issue and will be more hesitant to repeat the behavior. Mainly because people don't like to prove you right. Once they've been called out on something, they'll at least think twice before doing it again. They'll either remove themselves from you or they'll think twice about continuing those behaviors. Either way, it's a win-win for you.

Let me be clear here. There's not a 100% guarantee they won't ever repeat the hurtful behavior, but they do become more conscious of it and are more mindful of not repeating the negative behavior. It's very important you let the issue be known because again, you still communicate with them on a regular basis. At the very least this person will receive your letter, read it, and process it.

The point of the letter is not to get a reaction from the person or to expect a resolution for the issue. The purpose of writing the letter and sending it is to get the things hurting you off your chest and to release them so you can heal.

You might be saying to yourself, "There's no way in hell I'm sending this letter. I don't want to talk to them. I don't want to open this door. It's just not something I want to entertain." I get that.

Let me share something with you. I, for the first-time last year, had to take myself through this entire process and write a letter. I also had to fight with myself and argue with God about whether I should send the letter to the person who triggered me to need to write it. Ultimately, I was obedient and sent the letter.

Believe me, I know it's hard. However, I want you to trust me. Trust the process. More importantly, trust God's instruction if He directs you to send the letter after you pray about it.

With that said, when I wrote my letters earlier last year because of something that had hurt me, I started to see for myself how difficult it is to write the letters. It takes a lot out of you and it is tough. I had real fears when it came time to send the letter. I worried about how the person was going to perceive it and how they might react to it.

Pride is real. It will try to get in the way. I didn't want the person to think certain things, like I was still holding on to this. I didn't want her to think or to assume I still had feelings for her.

Let me pause here. Listen, if you've gone through some tough things with someone and now you're broken up, you don't deal with them, an ex-husband, ex-wife, ex-boyfriend/girlfriend, ex-whatever, there is nothing wrong with the fact that you may still love them.

There is a difference between loving them and being in a relationship with them. Yes, you may have reached a point in your life where you realize a relationship with them isn't going to work, but that doesn't mean you don't love them anymore.

A lot of times where people struggle is in fighting how they feel about someone. It's almost like you're mad at yourself for loving them. You're mad at yourself for still having feelings for them. When you do this, you're making matters worse for yourself. When you have genuine feelings for someone and you're trying to convince yourself to fight it, it's like fighting quicksand. The more you fight it, the deeper you sink. You make it more difficult for yourself to be at peace with the situation.

Don't fight yourself. Don't deny how you feel. Accept it for what it is. You can say, "You know what? Yes, I do love them. I do still care for them. But the relationship, it's not for me anymore. It's simply not going to work and that's okay." There are so many different things that can come up as to having fears and reasons why you won't want to send the letters.

However, it goes back to the point of this entire process, you must speak your truth. You can't be afraid of how someone is going to perceive or interpret it. It honestly doesn't matter. What matters is that you spoke your truth and that you give yourself permission to feel and express your feelings in an honest and loving manner. They can take it however they want. Who cares.

I know it's easier said than done, but it is what it is. You have to be able to stand on your truth regardless of their reaction. Think positive. There'll always be a worst-case scenario. However, you never know what can come from it. I've seen some amazing, beautiful things come out of this process. Let me give you an example.

A client came to me and one of the issues she was facing was a toxic relationship with her child's father. He was very verbally abusive. He would tell her, "I wish you would die." He would routinely speak all kinds of ill-will towards her. He wasn't being a good father either. It was just a very negative, unhealthy situation. When she came to me for coaching, we discussed the aspect of her relationship with her child's father. I suggested she complete the letter writing release exercise.

Her response was: "No. This isn't going to work. You don't understand. You don't know him. He's not going to read it. He's not going to do anything about it. It's not going to make a difference."

My response to her protests: "Listen, just trust me. Write the letters."

Finally, after going back and forth with her, she agreed to write the letters. As God is my witness, this is a true story. She wrote the letters and sent the second draft to him. He called her two or three days later having a complete meltdown.

Responding to her letter, he says to her verbatim, "I never realized how bad of a person I was to you."

Of course, she was shocked. She couldn't believe it! However, I wasn't surprised at all. I understood the power the letter would have once he sat down, read it, and really processed how he had negatively impacted her life.

Your letter can open the person's eyes in ways nothing else ever has.

No amount of complaining, lashing out, or the sum of their own personal negative experiences has ever made them really see their actions for what they are. When someone writes you a letter and again, isn't attacking you, isn't lashing out at you, but just fully expressing their emotions—understand there is a difference between lashing out and simply sharing with someone how they made you feel, how they impacted your life—when you come at it from this angle, it can have amazing effects.

I'm not going to sit here and say I can guarantee that if you send your letters, they're going to allow you to reconcile with every single person or that you're going to see amazing things happen in every situation.

However, whether they respond or not, no matter how they take it, the only thing that matters is you getting free from the previously unresolved toxic energy and healing.

WHEN NOT TO SEND THE LETTER

Now, there are a couple of exceptions to sending a letter. Of course, if the person is deceased then sending the letter is completely off the table. I suggest burning the letter instead.

Take the piece of paper(s) and without folding them, hold a lighter to one corner, over the sink or outdoors, so you don't risk injuries or burning down your house, and watch the letter be consumed by the flame. This is going to help bring closure to the emotions and feelings attached to the person and the experience.

Once you've burned the letter, don't look back. Send up a prayer of peace and move on.

Another exception to sending the letter is if this person is generally a threat to your safety. If you're dealing with individuals who are physically abusive, who have threatened your life, or any other situations where your safety is in danger, don't take the risk of sending the letter and making an already dangerous situation, worse.

Do I think it's possible for the letter, even in that type of scenario, to have a positive effect? Absolutely. However, this is where it's imperative you pray, talk to God, and get divine direction.

I don't want you to put yourself in harm's way. I also don't know the details of your specific situation. Go to God and follow God's instructions of whether you should send the letter.

The other exception to not sending the letter and this is very common with a lot of people, the letter can't be sent because the letter is written to God. It's very common that God makes it on your "Who Hurt Me List." Many people are upset at God. Many people hold resentment towards God for various reasons.

Listen, you don't have to lie about it. You don't have to be in denial about it because God knows you're pissed off. God knows you don't like Him. I don't care who you are, how old you are, or how much of a believer you've been all these years. Many, if not all of us, have had a moment or moments where we were/are a little pissed at God.

I'm not going to say its human nature, but it is more common than many would believe or want to acknowledge. So, if God made your list then even though you can't send the letter, writing a letter to God is still a really good idea. Let it all out. Scream, curse, put it all in the letter. Go through the same process if God made it on your "Who Hurt Me List" because it will help you release. Once you finish writing both drafts of your letters to God, I recommend you pray over the letters. After you pray over them, burn the second draft as well.

As a recap, depending on whether God has released you to send the letter(s), the final step in getting things off your chest is taking the second and final draft of your letter and either mailing it or burning it.

I want to remind you again that if you're sending your letters do so without expectation. Be open to reconciliation, however, don't expect it. The only person you have control over is you. You did your part and you received the benefits of the release. The rest is up to God and the other person.

Once they've received your letter, had time to process it and reach out, you'll have had enough time to prepare for what is essential in all healthy relationships that you want to sustain over the long-term, forgiveness.

MY EXPERIENCE

I'll be completely honest and transparent with you here. I've written my own letter to God before. Certain things I've experienced in my life caused me at times to be really pissed off and mad at God. At times I found myself cursing God out. You may read that and say, "How dare you?"

Listen, it is what it is. It's how I felt. I'm not going to run away from it. I'm not going to lie about it. I'm going to be real about it. Because again, I can't overcome or resolve my own issues if I'm not going to be truthful about how I feel. God already knows anyway. There is no point in hiding it.

Writing the letters allowed me to process through the anger I had towards God. I was able to work through the negative emotions and found this honest release was needed for me to experience the close relationship I have with God today.

Again, it doesn't make sense to hold on to anything no matter who it involves. In times of hurt, heartbreak, and pain we need God more than ever. However, unforgiveness toward God will make it seem like God's far away from you. I want you to know that's never the case. God is waiting for you to be honest with yourself and Him about everything. He wants to take away the burdens you're carrying and give you peace in return.

PART III

DAILY PRACTICES, EXPERIENCING DEEPER

Healing

PRACTICING FORGIVENESS IS KEY

The next step in my healing method is practicing forgiveness. However, before you can practice forgiveness, it's important that we get rid of any misconceptions you may have about forgiveness first.

Many people think that forgiving someone is a decision made once, in your mind, and that's it. Another common misconception people have is they equate forgiveness with acceptance. However, when you approach forgiveness from these angles, you set yourself up for a constant internal battle and you cause yourself to suffer more as a result.

What does it mean to really forgive? First, let me point out that the word "forgive" is a transitive verb. A transitive verb is a verb that requires two or more objects because one is being acted upon. A verb is a word that shows action, meaning it's something you do, not think or feel. The definition of "forgive" according to *Merriam-Webster* is 1. to cease to feel resentment against (an offender). 2. To give up resentment of or claim to requital for. 3. To grant relief from payment of.

All three of these definitions illustrate that it is in the power of the person forgiving to make the decision to act.

The opposite of forgive is to resent.

Let me be clear here. Forgiving someone, doesn't' mean you're saying what they did is okay, acceptable, or that you're going to let it slide. Not true at all. Understand that forgiveness doesn't mean what happened is okay. You're not co-signing the experience or person. You're not giving them a pass or condoning what they've done. This is one of the big misconceptions about forgiveness.

Forgiveness is another form of release. When you forgive someone, you're saying, "I'm no longer going to hold on to the negative feelings and energy of a situation or the anger I have towards a person any longer."

Everything is forgivable.

However, some things are unacceptable and there is a difference. You might be saying, "Oh, hell no. There are some things that are unforgivable. There's no way I'm going to forgive someone who raped me, molested my child, murdered my family member, or broke my heart."

However, you can and should forgive them. By the time you're done reading this book I pray you'll be able to forgive everyone who has ever hurt you, no matter how painful the situation might have been.

"Forgiving someone is for your benefit first."

Even though you've probably heard this saying a million times before and it sounds cliché, it's the truth. I said it again for your remembrance and in case you are a rare soul who's never heard it before.

Another reason you may be struggling with the idea of forgiving someone is that you've internalized what the individual did to you. As I mentioned earlier on, hurt people, hurt people. Many people are trying to defend or protect themselves and that may sound crazy, but again, hurt people, hurt people.

Forgiveness is a choice. Your choice. It's your decision to forgive someone, which empowers you to take back control over your life, your emotions, and your healing. The act of forgiveness simply means, "I'm not going to keep holding on to this." Unforgiveness is like holding poison in your hands and waiting for the other person to drink it. Whether you realize it or not, you're the person most affected and further damaged by unforgiveness.

The person who hurt you probably isn't suffering because you didn't forgive them. So, if you think not forgiving someone is revenge or payback for their wrong toward you, it's not. Plain and simple. Let me make it plainer for you if you're among the stubborn bunch.

Unforgiveness is suicide. You're literally killing yourself.

When I say, "killing," that's not an exaggeration or an extreme word to use. A lack of forgiveness and holding on to bad energy turns into toxic emotional stress and that stress is eating away at you from the inside out. We've already talked about how unresolved emotional stress can cause all kinds of ailments and trigger diseases that can potentially shorten your lifespan. Again, it's not an exaggeration, it's the reality of it. A large part of removing stress from your life is found in forgiveness.

Forgiveness is for your freedom. It's for your peace. It's for your overall better health and well-being.

Let's use the example of being cheated on. When you're in a relationship with someone and they cheat on you, if you're like, "I can never forgive them." A big part of why you're refusing to forgive them is because you think that forgiving them means you accept their behavior or need to remain in a relationship with them. Wrong.

Forgiving them doesn't mean either of these things. The reality is that the person may have never belonged in your life. That person may have been someone you should have never entertained romantically. Forgiveness allows you to recognize and say to yourself, "We aren't best for each other. This friendship is not going to work anymore. This is not someone I can go talk to. This is not someone I can interact and engage with." Even when you come to those conclusions, you can still forgive.

I mentioned it in an earlier chapter, you can't afford to take other people's actions personally.

What people do and say many times has nothing to do with you. It is a result of their own hurt. Taking their hurt and internalizing it, is like walking around with this huge weight on your shoulders and allowing it to continuously beat you down. Taking offense and carrying unforgiveness, whether you realized it or not, has been deteriorating you mentally, emotionally and spiritually. Practicing forgiveness toward others will free you of that.

Ultimately, there are two steps to forgiveness. The first step is forgiving the other person. The second step is forgiving yourself.

God instructs us regarding forgiving others in the Bible. *"If you forgive those who sin against you, your heavenly Father will forgive you. But if you refuse to forgive others, your Father will not forgive your sins."* Matthew 6:14-15, NLT

Forgiveness is something that believers must embrace from a spiritual perspective, always, if we expect to have God's forgiveness. Think about that for a moment.

Listen, we all make mistakes. We all do things we're not supposed to do. I'm sure we all have things we're not necessarily proud of or could've handled better. God always forgives us because He knows the good in us. God knows we're human and imperfect. He knows that we're going to make mistakes. We need to take God's example and apply it to our understanding in our interactions with each other.

Realize that people are going to fall short. People are going to do things to hurt you. However, you can't control other people's actions. You can only your own. Also, within your control is the power to forgive them and move forward. You can learn from the situation and make better decisions in the future.

The second step in practicing forgiveness is forgiving yourself. I think this may be an even bigger obstacle for many people.

Forgiving yourself means you need to acknowledge the issues and mistakes of your past you may be holding onto. As a result of past mistakes, you might not trust yourself anymore. You might have begun to constantly beat yourself up about things. You might have developed low self-esteem or low self-worth as a result. All because you're holding unforgiveness towards yourself from past experiences.

If you've experienced rejection, abandonment, sexual abuse, or the consequences of your own bad decisions that put you in uncomfortable situations, you might hold unforgiveness toward yourself. The list of reasons why we hold unforgiveness toward ourselves is endless.

Let me pause quickly here. You might be shocked by the sexual abuse mention above. You might be thinking, "Well, why would sexual abuse be on the list because that's an act done against someone else?"

You're right. However, the reality is that some survivors of sexual abuse hold their own guilt in the situation. They often wonder if they did anything to provoke or deserve it. Sometimes the abuser tries to convince them of accepting responsibility or blame and then they hold on to that. In these situations, it's easy to hold things over your own head as to why it happened, but ultimately, you don't need to hold anything over your head where this is concerned. If you have, release it and forgive yourself.

Once again, forgiveness of any kind is your choice to make. Let it go. In the case of abuse of any kind, you never deserve that type of experience and it's important to rid yourself of the weight of any guilt.

When it comes to normal every day experiences, remember, you're human. You're going to make mistakes. The key is to learn from your mistakes and begin to understand how to process them correctly. Doing so will allow you to grow and move forward in a healthy way.

The reality is that practicing forgiveness isn't a snap-of-the-fingers type of thing. You can go through all the exercises I'm giving you and take all the steps. You can forgive the other people involved and yourself tomorrow and three days later something will happen that triggers you. Suddenly, you're back in a negative headspace. You're back to beating yourself up. Holding on to past issues or feeling some-kind-of-way about what someone did to you in the past.

In that moment you need to do what I call *Practicing the Forgiveness*. You must keep yourself from dwelling and falling too deep into that negative thinking. Stop and remind yourself, "No, I won't go back there. I forgave them and I forgave myself. What's done is done. I'm moving forward." That's what I mean when I say, *Practicing the Forgiveness*. You need to do that every time you start to think negatively, beat yourself up, or go back to a bad mental or emotional place because it's going to happen.

It takes a while for us to get everything out of our system and for us to truly flush it out of our spirit. Practicing forgiveness is ongoing. You need to be consistent with it. If you keep practicing and fighting those negative moments, reminding yourself, "I forgave them. I forgive me. What's done is done. I'm moving forward."

When you do this consistently, you're going to notice you get triggered a lot less. You'll start to notice that the previous thoughts and negative feelings associated with the person or experience have less of an impact on you. You'll reach a point where you're no longer phased by it at all.

Practicing the Forgiveness is all about continuously keeping your mind on the fact that you're moving forward, that you've forgiven everyone involved, and you're not going to dwell on the negativity anymore.

Too many times we allow ourselves to get pulled back into negative thinking and emotions. Do your best not to allow this to happen. You must work to do better. You've got to fight to move forward. Know that it's going to be so worth it when you do.

Again, forgiveness is a practice. It's a constant decision you make with your heart not to hold on to unforgiveness. Remember, forgiveness is for your sake not the other person's. Think of forgiveness like other things you do to improve your overall health and wellness. Like practicing yoga, meditation, a workout regimen, etc. All these things require you to make a conscious decision and effort to stick with them. The more you do them, the better results you have from the practice, the better shape you'll be in as you continue practicing.

Begin to look at forgiveness in much the same way. Practicing forgiveness is for your benefit and for your overall improved health and wellness.

CHANGE YOUR MINDSET

The negative experiences we go through in life eventually start to shape our perception of the world around us. I want you to ask yourself a question. "Have I become cynical as a result of the hurt I've experienced in my life?"

Our experiences begin to pull us in one direction or another, sometimes good, sometimes bad. It's easy to begin to attach a negative perception to your present and future experiences based off your past. In order to move out of the negative place that you've dwelled in, a place that hasn't gotten you the results you want, a place that hasn't brought you any happiness or peace, you're going to have to be willing to change your mindset.

A large part of the battle of getting the love you deserve starts in your mind. It starts with how you view things, how you think, how you act, and how you behave. When you understand that you always have a choice, you'll be able to conquer this and move on from your hurt.

When it comes to your past hurts and disappointments, 9 times out of 10, you'll use your past to assess your present situation. Doing this paralyzes you. It hinders you from making sound decisions in your present life including, your relationships, career, health, etc. It's important to pay attention and be mindful of how you're looking at the people, places, and things around you after you've been hurt.

You might be thinking, "Why is this a bad thing? Isn't it helping me stay away from danger? Won't it help me stay away from people who will just do me more harm?"

No, it won't. A lot of times, people aren't out to do you harm in the first place. The hypothetical situations you're "protecting" yourself from may not be any danger to you at all. Projecting negativity onto current situations because of what you've already been through can cause you to miss your blessings.

A perfect example of this is when you have a negative experience with one person from a certain religious background, nationality, race, or gender. Once this happens, moving forward, it's easy to project your negative perception onto all people associated with that group, which is not healthy. Doing this almost always creates more problems for all involved. However, you can do away with the projecting and the false sense of protection by changing your mindset.

The first step in *Changing Your Mindset* is to identify your negative perceptions. You must be willing to recognize what causes your perception of things and if they're positive or negative.

For example, let's say you've been robbed by someone of a different race. I'm not going to pick a specific one. You can pick one for yourself. Let's say a person from this race robbed you. Now every time you're around people of this race you become uncomfortable. You become more guarded and you start to project negativity and fear toward this group of people.

Ultimately, you're creating a very unhealthy environment when you're in the vicinity of a person who's associated with this group. I want you to really consider this example. I'm just giving one example, but there are various things you may have gone through that have caused you to have a negative perception about certain types of people, places, or things as a result.

If you're a woman who's been cheated on by a man, you might have the negative perception now that all men will cheat. If you're a man who's been cheated on by a woman, you might have the negative perception that now all women can't be trusted.

It's important you take some time now to start to identify these things. Grab your workbook and start to write them down. Ask yourself, "What are my negative perceptions about people, places, and situations?"

Let's take it even further than just relationships. If you're thinking, "Oh, well. You know what? The country I'm living in doesn't want me to succeed or doesn't allow me to go further in life." I get it. I'm not saying there aren't real limitations out there, real biases, and real obstacles. However, it doesn't serve you to keep holding onto your negative perceptions. Dwelling on things you can't control, and that lot of times may not be the case or at least not to the extent you think they are, keep you stuck and unable to embrace the positive.

Take some time now to write down some things you think negatively about. Again, ask yourself, "What do I have negative perceptions of?" Start to identify these things.

The next step in *Changing Your Mindset* is to take those negative perceptions you identified and find the good. For example, if one of your negative perceptions is "all men cheat or are dogs." Well, let's start to look at some of the men who, at least to your knowledge, have been loyal. Consider the fact that *even if you can't see them, there are good men out there.*

The same thing applies if you're a man who has experienced some unhealthy relationships with women. Start to focus on the positive.

Again, a lot of times, our inability to see the good is not because the good doesn't exist, it's just that we're so fixated on the negative, we're not allowing ourselves to shift our focus. Begin to acknowledge and embrace the positive that does in fact exist in your life.

The reality is that in embracing the positive, you now open yourself up to being vulnerable. There's this fear of, "Oh, the minute I begin to trust or think positive about a situation or person, the bad will come. A bad situation is going to happen to me again. It's better just to think negatively, be prepared, and brace myself for it so that I don't get hit as hard by it."

Wrong. You may not get hit at all. You may be hit but not by any particular situation, but by your own fears, your own issues, your own negative energy. You're hurting yourself one way or another by doing this. I tell people all the time, the same walls you built to protect you are the same walls blocking your blessings. You're holding yourself back in life, whether you realize it or not because of your negative perceptions. Again, start focusing on the good. Start looking for and finding the good in every situation.

Just like with practicing forgiveness, *Changing Your Mindset* requires practice. Practice makes better. We're aiming for progress here, not perfection. When you start to look at things in a negative light, stop yourself.

Let me give you a personal example of this. Let's just say a celebrity on the Internet does something I don't like or that rubs me the wrong way. I might go into a negative thought. When I do, I stop myself. I say, "Wait a minute. I don't know them. I know nothing about them. They may be a wonderful, great person. You know what? I wish them the best."

Seriously, I literally do that. I catch myself when I start to think negative of people, things and situations. I remind myself of the good, even if I don't know for sure that the good exists or is in them.

However, honestly, I believe good is present in all of us. I believe people who seem to just be horrible people are just hurt and extremely damaged people. I think that most people in this world, if not everyone, is ultimately good. Unfortunately, that good might be suppressed, pushed to the side, or dismissed due to all the hurt and pain they've experienced. As a result, they project out into the world, their pain. Since I believe good exists in everyone, I'm willing to look for the good in a person or believe in it no matter what.

Start to practice this in your own life. In everyday situations when you find yourself thinking negatively, or holding onto unhealthy perceptions of things, especially when it's specifically connected to a negative experience you've had, catch yourself. Try to look for the positive somewhere in it. You don't want to start projecting this negative perception on everything else. Really work on changing that.

Say to yourself, "Nope, I won't choose negativity. There is good all around me, even if I don't see it and have yet to experience it. There are good men. There are good women. I do have the opportunity to do better in my life. I do have the opportunity to be more successful. I can make more happen for myself."

Whatever the negative perception may be, remind yourself of the good. The more you do it, the more it becomes second nature and you won't have to think about it at all. You're default response will be to see the positive first. You won't be so quick to go to the negative anymore and you'll allow yourself to be able to experience more of the positive life has to offer as a result.

TRUST GOD, NOT PEOPLE

The last point I want to make is to learn to trust your Spirit. I do a lot of touring and I get booked for a lot of different speaking events and one of the things I talk about at my events is the need to trust God, not people. Intuition, gut instinct, and spiritual discernment is present within all of us.

Think about that for a second.

When you don't just rely on what your eyes see, your ears hear, or what you want to process in your mind, when you start to listen from within, you start to gain a better understanding of the people and events that occur in life. Sometimes you don't know why something happens. You might not be able to make sense of it. However, if you listen and tune in, your gut, your Spirit, will reveal the truth to you.

We're all capable of being shady. To trust people, you need to really accept that we're all human. We're all going to make mistakes. We're all going to end up hurting people no matter how good or holy we feel we are. It makes no difference. We're all flawed at the end of the day.

When we hold people to a high expectation, we're going to, most of the time, be let down. Mainly because as humans we're too flawed to uphold and live up to the expectations put on us by others.

By shifting your focus to trusting your Spirit, you begin to trust God and not people. You're able to allow yourself to navigate this world with a much more, I hate to use the word, realistic, but in my perception, a more realistic expectation.

Again, for me, I've realized, not to expect anything of anyone because I know everyone can fall short. I can fall short. It doesn't necessarily surprise me when someone hurts me. I understand that if they've done something to hurt me or wrong me that it's not about me, there's something deeper going on with them.

By having that perception and understanding, it allows me to be able to not internalize things as much. It allows me to hold on to positivity, love, and a better outlook on the situation. I don't get caught up in the falseness of putting high expectations on people who are going to most likely let me down.

It happens a lot, even with our parents. I've worked with people who are still mad at their parents because in their minds, "their parents should have known better." Listen, your parents are human beings too. Again, if we go deeper and look at this from a spiritual perspective, the Bible tells us simply, *"Do not put your trust in princes, in human beings, who cannot save. Blessed are those whose help is the God of Jacob; whose hope is in the Lord their God."* Psalm 146:3-5 NIV

Putting 100% of your trust in anyone is just not realistic. It's not fair to them. It's not fair to you. It doesn't mean you should go around not trusting people. It just means you need to understand that things will happen sometimes to cause people to fall short. Lead with understanding and patience, instead of offensiveness and the spirit of unforgiveness.

Sure, you should have standards. We all have standards. It's healthy to have a place where we draw a line in the sand that says, "Hey, if you're not going to uphold these standards and what I need from you, then I'm not going to entertain you." That's fair. That's reasonable. However, to be so hurt and angry when people don't do what we wanted them to do, it doesn't get us anywhere. It just puts you in a bad place. It just sends you into a negative space. It's not healthy and it's unnecessary.

When you start to put more trust in God and your Spirit rather than in people, you'll be able to make better decisions. You'll be able to live a healthier, happier life. You'll be able to avoid a lot of the hurt and damage that occurs when people let you down. By doing this you'll avoid the need to have to heal in the first place.

CONCLUSION

Congratulations! You made it through. I want you to take a moment and just celebrate yourself and all the progress you've made so far. You've laid the groundwork by beginning to work through the exercises I've shared with you throughout this book. You're closer to healing and finding the love you seek.

I know it was a lot of work. I know that if you completed the exercises while reading, it took a lot out of you, and it wasn't the easiest process to go through. However, I want you to know that the methods I laid out for you in this book are an extension of what I used to achieve healing myself. I wanted you to have access to the different levels and benefits of self-healing that I've paid therapists and coaches to help me through in the past.

In addition to working through the different processes I shared with you in this book, getting myself to a healed place, also took me going to God consistently in prayer to heal from past hurts. I also made the decision to remove myself from dating and romantic relationships when I was going through my healing process. I practiced abstinence as well. It was a huge help in allowing me to focus on me and getting a better understanding of who I am as a person.

Working through my healing process, practicing abstinence, and spending more alone time with God helped me begin to understand the people around me. Getting closer to God really helped me to heal and to get to a healthier place in my life. I really started to see things differently and this allowed me to begin helping other people.

Sure, I had a therapist help me along the way, but it still required me to do the work necessary to attain the healing I needed. However, I was willing to do whatever it took to get me to a healthier place in life.

I want you to do the same. I want you to know you're not a victim of what life throws at you. You are a victor. You can conquer anything and overcome it all, but you must embrace the strength you have within you to do it. You need to be willing to take the necessary steps. You must be willing to make the necessary sacrifices and embrace the necessary changes in order to receive what you deserve in life.

My hope is that while reading this book, you started to see the light at the end of your "I'm healing" tunnel. I hope you started to notice the positive changes that occur when you do your part. My hope is you've started to get your heart back to where it belongs, to a place where it can love and be loved. To a place where it is open to vulnerability. To a place where it doesn't fear being hurt, but understands the truth about getting hurt in this life we live in.

Again, being hurt is not something you can escape from. It's something you've now learned how to manage and handle better. With practice you'll learn how to process, overcome, and swiftly bounce back from hurtful experiences. Remember hurt is a teacher. With every lesson, you grow in wisdom and learn how to adjust and handle the next obstacle.

You may be asking yourself, "I thought this book was supposed to be about finding love after heartbreak. Where's the finding love part?"

Healing comes before finding love. Healing is the first and most important step to take in finding love after heartbreak. This is just Volume I of a two-part series. I broke it up because I need you to focus on achieving the healing you must experience first.

I can't tell you how many people come to me, rushing to find love without properly addressing the pain of their past. They're rushing to get that relationship and figure out how to solve all their dating issues. The reality is they're not doing the necessary groundwork first. They're not laying the right foundation for relationship success. The proper foundation starts with your healing, with addressing and resolving all the past hurts and disappointments that you've left unresolved.

I broke things up because I need you to be able to properly digest this information by itself before going back out here and looking for love. I wanted to make sure you're able to take the time out to go through each step in the Stephan Speaks Healing Method and do the exercises I shared with you.

It's very easy to get distracted by the desire to be in a relationship and skip ahead. If I would've gone through the receiving love from a romantic standpoint, as well as from a self-love standpoint, which I'm going to dive into in Volume 2 of *Finding Love After Heartbreak*, it would've been very easy to glance over the healing process altogether.

We often want the results without the work. However, it doesn't work that way in life or in love. You get back what you put in. I want you to have it all and to be able to sustain the relationship of your dreams once you're blessed with it.

For that to happen you need to take this time to focus and home in on you. I want you to make sure you do your work first. Focus on the work that needs to happen within you. This is possibly the biggest missing piece of the puzzle. When it comes to getting that great, healthy, amazing relationship, it takes two great, healthy, amazing, whole individuals coming together as one.

The process I laid out in this book is not limited to reaping the benefits in only romantic relationships either. As I've mentioned already, my healing method is going to help you have better relationships with your family, parents, friends, co-workers, in business, you name it. Going through my healing process is going to help you connect better with people in all areas of your life.

I honestly don't want you to get so locked into the romantic aspect that you miss the main reason and benefit your healing is going to have. Your healing is going to help you have a better relationship with yourself because that's the other missing foundational piece.

You must love yourself first. Self-love is a necessity. It's not selfish. If you're not good to you, you're not going to be good to anyone else. You're going to be wearing yourself out trying to give yourself to the wrong people, for the wrong reasons, producing the wrong results. It's important to break the cycle. I don't want you to be someone who continues to ignore your issues or suppress your negative emotions or unresolved pain.

Again, go through this entire process as many times as needed. If you started and didn't finish certain exercises, go back to them and do the rest of what you need to do. Do not make excuses or try to convince yourself that nothing's wrong or your past certain things. You can do something about your issues. Make the decision to resolve them for good.

I told you at the beginning of this healing journey, to hold out your hand so I could catch you. The *Stephan Speaks Healing Method* is me extending my hand to you, stopping you from continuing your freefall. However, it's up to you to let go of what you've been holding onto in order to embrace what you desire in its place.

Make room.

You're worth it. You deserve it.

My prayer for you:

I pray that God's love has washed over you completely on this healing journey. I pray that a proper foundation has now been laid and as you continue to implement all the steps I shared, you're going to be ready for the next level I'll share with you in Volume 2. I pray God restores your brokenness. I pray He renews your mind and strengthens your spirit. I pray you'll begin to see yourself as God sees you, fearfully and wonderfully made, not lacking anything. I pray you will begin to realize you are deserving of everything good. By faith, it is so. In Jesus name, *Amen*.

AUTHOR DISCLAIMER

The stories, characters, and scenarios used as examples throughout the book are based off real situations but have been fictionalized to protect the identities of my clients.

Any names or likeness to actual persons, either living or dead, is strictly coincidental. This book is designed to provide information and motivation to readers. Neither the publisher nor author shall be liable for any physical, psychological, emotional, financial, or commercial damages, including, but not limited to, special, incidental, consequential or other damages.

Every person is different and the advice and strategies contained herein may not be suitable for your situation. Our views and rights are the same: You are responsible for your own choices, actions, and results.

About The Author

$\mathscr{S}$tephan Labossiere is *the* "Relationship Guy." An authority on real love, real talk, real relationships. The brand *Stephan Speaks* is synonymous with happier relationships and healthier people around the globe. For more than a decade, Stephan has committed himself to breaking down relationship barriers, pushing past common facades, and exposing the truth. It is his understanding of REAL relationships that has empowered millions of people, clients and readers alike, to create their best lives by being able to experience and sustain greater love.

Seen, heard, and chronicled in national and international media outlets including; the *Tom Joyner Morning Show*, *The Examiner*, *ABC*, *GQ*, and *Huffington Post Live*. The certified life & relationship coach, speaker, and award winning, bestselling author is the voice that the world tunes into for answers to their difficult relationship woes. From understanding the opposite sex, to navigating the paths and avoiding the pitfalls of relationships and self-growth, Stephan's relationship advice and insight helps countless men and women overcome the situations hindering them from achieving an authentically amazing life.

Stephan is highly sought-after because he is able to dispel the myths of relationship breakdowns and obstacles–platonic, romantic, and otherwise—with fervor and finesse. His signature style, relatability, and passion make international audiences sit up and pay attention.

"My message is simple: life and relationships require truth. The willingness to speak truth and the bravery to acknowledge truth is paramount."

Are you listening?

Enough said.

JUST RELEASED BY
𝒮TEPHAN 𝒮PEAKS

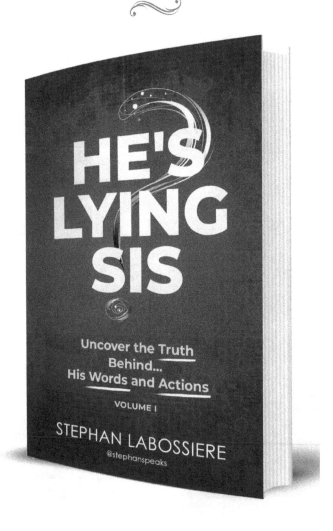

www.HesLyingSis.com

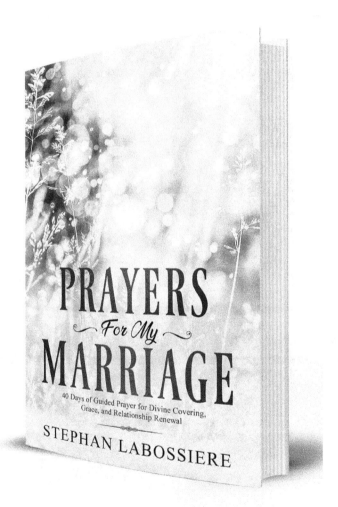

www.PrayersForMyMarriageBook.com

POPULAR BOOKS BY
Stephan Speaks

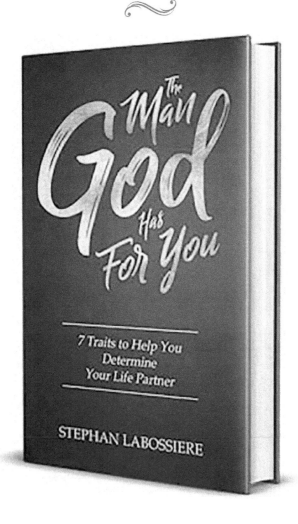

www.TheManGodHasForMe.com

www.GetAManToCherishYou.com

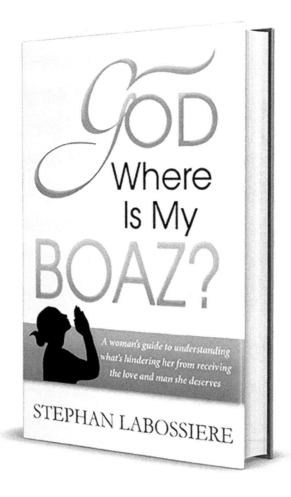

www.BetterMarriageBetterLoving.com

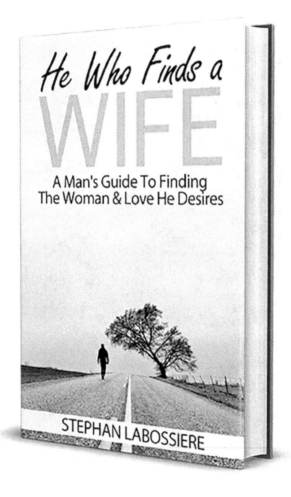

WHAT CLIENTS & READERS ARE SAYING ABOUT TEPHAN PEAKS!

INSIGHT & HONESTY

Stephan Labossiere has a rare blend of compassion, insight and honesty. He understands relationships, and is a supportive partner and guide on your journey to creating the love and life you want.

—Lisa Marie Bobby

HE'S FUN & LOVING

You hear people saying you must love yourself first, so you can attract the love of your life. This is what I wanted, and for me I did not quite know what this meant until I worked with Stephan. His work is fun, he is very loving, and you get results fast, because he sees very clearly what is going on. I truly recommend signing up for his coaching!

—Dominique, *Paris, France*

A JOY TO WORK WITH

As someone who has studied the role of men and women in relationships in our society for many years, it has been a joy to get to know and work with Stephan. His knowledge and candid from the heart writings and speaking on the topic of relationships are a breath of fresh air and sure to take you and your relationships to a more authentic and loving way of being.

–Tom Preston

More relationship resources can be found at www.StephanSpeaks.com/shop/

You can also follow me on Twitter & Instagram: **@StephanSpeaks** or find me on Facebook under **"Stephan Speaks Relationships"**

CPSIA information can be obtained
at www.ICGtesting.com
Printed in the USA
BVHW072355290720
584956BV00005B/5